LOSE YOUR SH*T

LOSE YOUR SH⚡T

SHED YOUR STRESS, UNLEASH YOUR SUPERPOWERS, CRUSH YOUR BUSINESS

JODI HADSELL

Lose Your Sh*t
Shed Your Stress, Ignite Your Superpowers, Crush Your Business

ISBN: 979-8-6838-8698-1

Cover Design: Jodi Hadsell
Editing: Bethany Davis and Moriah Richard
Author Photo Credit: Dee Hill / Dee Hill Photography

DEDICATION

This one is for Rudy. Thank you for your undying support, love and friendship, and for trusting me.

CONTENTS

lose one's sh*t
verb

Definition

(idiomatic) To lose one's temper.
(idiomatic) To have a sudden burst of emotion, regardless of the type of feeling.

(idiomatic,) To break down in laughter.

Antonym

hold it together

CHAPTER 1: WHAT IS YOUR DEAL?

"We live in the deep sea, surrounded by pressure that could kill us in an instant, with no access to the surface world, that is our natural home."

– G. R. Matthews

Are you tired of being "the boss" but not really having time or energy to truly lead? Are you tired of being involved in every decision? Are you tired of being responsible for everyone in your life? Of feeling like a pressure cooker about to blow? Is your reputation slipping because you are having a hard time keeping it together? Are you overwhelmed, anxious, and exhausted? Like any minute you could lose your sh*t or lose your business?

Well, welcome to being an entrepreneur!

We are all under lots of pressure in this day and age, but as an entrepreneur, you have an extra layer of pressure because you are carrying a burden that is unlike any other. In some instances, you are responsible for your business, the ideas, sales, service, operations, productivity, complaints, legal stuff, and on and on. The buck stops at you. And that is not including your personal life, where you may be responsible for a maintaining a residence, a spouse or partner, kids, aging parents, siblings, ex-spouses, and so on. That is a very heavy burden to carry. It's a lonely struggle when no one in your life truly understands it.

You just wish the world would stop for a week or even a day so you could catch up. You would love to take a break or slow down. But that is not possible, and you don't remember the last time you took time off for a vacation. You tried counseling but that was not really for you. You feel like the walking dead and are headed for zombieland and do not see a way out. You tried eating right and working out, but that is not really doing the trick, is it? You are constantly worried about money and your responsibilities

– you cannot disappoint the people who depend on you. Failure is not an option. You feel uncertain and vulnerable, but you dare not let anyone know.

Does any of those describe you? If so, you have come to the right place. You are not alone.

The Cost of Being a Pressure Cooker

Many leaders and entrepreneurs struggle with chronic or toxic stress. When we are in a state of stress, it impedes our decisions, our ability to act and move forward. It disempowers us as leaders. In addition chronic stress can lead to many health issues, including headaches, heart problems, high blood pressure, suppressed immune response, sleep disturbances, digestive issues, structural issues, and so on. Prolonged exposure to chronic stress (that is, toxic stress) can lead to memory loss, anxiety, irritability, anger issues, depression, substance abuse, social withdrawal, weight gain, insomnia, suicidal thoughts, or worse.

I know because that described me. I was a "zombie entrepreneur" and I experienced toxic stress for many years. And it almost killed me. That is high price to pay for entrepreneurship.

What if I told you that I discovered a way out of the entrepreneurial zombieland? It has worked for me and my clients. Fasten your seat belts because you are getting ready to embark on a journey that is enlightening, scary, fun, and life-altering. Let's go!

CHAPTER 2: MY STRESS-DEFEATING JOURNEY

"These mountains that you are carrying, you were only supposed to climb."

– Najwa Zebian

My stress journey is a long one. For most of my childhood, I lived in fear. My dad was a raging and controlling narcissist, my mother was depressed, my brother was abusive, and my sister was a bully. I had "everything I could ever want" (as my father used to remind me), but peace of mind was not one of them. "Acting out" or expressing any kind of emotion was not allowed in my family. Anxiety, worry, and stress were just part of who I was. It was like it was hardwired into me at a very young age. At age 11 my mother finally divorced my father and he and my brother moved out, so things got better. That is when I started to kind of have a normal life. Or at least that is what I thought.

But one fateful day when I was 14, everything changed. My sister accidentally ran over and killed our puppy. We were devastated. My father came over shortly afterward and got really upset with me for crying over "some stupid puppy." He kept telling me to "stop crying." I lost it and yelled at him and told him that he could not control me. He was not having that so he hit me. Really hard. With the back of his hand on my face. So hard that I flew across the room into the bathroom and hit my head on the tile floor and passed out for several seconds. My mouth was bleeding. My mother ran in and kicked him out of the house. I'll never forget getting up, dizzy and in shock, having that metallic blood taste in my mouth and looking in the mirror and seeing the imprint of his initial ring on my left cheek. That day I stopped emoting. Completely. I didn't cry, get mad, or get much of anything after that... for 15 years. I held *everything* in for 15 years. Can you imagine a teenage girl not crying? Not getting upset or angry? Well, that was me. For the next 15 years, I was like a zombie, just going through the motions of life with no real emotion. Meanwhile, the stress was building up in my body day by day.

Fast forward 15 years. I was making good money being a good "corporate zombie," working in corporate learning and development for a large technology firm. I was super "healthy" – meaning eating healthfully, exercising, working out with a personal trainer, having a busy social life, and dating. Everything seemed great on paper. And then the guy I had been dating dumped me and I just *lost* it. Over a breakup with someone I didn't even like that much. I believe my body had had just about enough of holding "it" in and that was the last straw. I didn't understand why I was "over-reacting," so I went to my family doctor and told him that I thought I was going crazy. My anxiety was overwhelming, I couldn't concentrate, I couldn't sleep, and I was gaining weight. He recommended a psychotherapist.

As soon as I went into therapy, the dam finally broke. For the first three months in therapy, I cried. Hysterically. Every day. All of those unshed tears were still inside me, causing so much stress and anxiety. I learned then that all unexpressed emotions (emotions that you do not process *out* of your body) stay in your body like energetic, emotional residue and wreak havoc, creating all kinds of physical and emotional health problems. After months of crying, I got so much better. Then came the anger. The boiling anger that I had not let out for years was popping up to surface with no problem, but I didn't know how to deal with it. So my therapist suggested "anger therapy." In her office she had a punching bag and a baseball bat, and she told me to "go for it," which included screaming, yelling, cursing, whatever needed to come out, and beating the bag with the bat over and over. It was amazing! Such a release. Freedom. She encouraged me to get a bat for home and use on my bed and do my anger therapy regularly. I did. But it was a bit tricky as I had pets and I lived in an apartment building. Practicing this scared my dog and disturbed my neighbors so I could not practice it as fully as I needed it. But when I did practice it on a regular basis, it felt amazing. It helped with my stress, anxiety, anger, and surprisingly kept my weight in check.

I stayed healthy like that for several years. I got into meditation and achieved every single goal I put in front of me with no problem. I was completely in flow with my life. Then I moved to San Francisco where I started my own business. The business was very successful (at least financially) for four years. But I happened to choose a business partner who was a carbon copy of my controlling, raging narcissist father! Imagine that. She triggered all of my old patterns and I basically became that teenager again – living in fear, holding everything in, not letting anything out, not standing up for myself, not setting boundaries, letting her run all over me, anxious all the time, not sleeping, and shutdown. I stopped all the practices that I had been doing for the last few years. I kept thinking, "If I can only get ahead, *then* I can get back to taking care of myself." I stopped working out, eating right, meditating, and had no social life. I thought for sure that I was either going to lose my sh*t or lose my business. I went back into psychotherapy, but it didn't help. My business became everything. I became a workaholic, working 80-100 hours a week, and I gained 50 pounds and lost half my hair. We ended our partnership after four years of misery and I paid her a lot of money to go away. Then right after that, the industry tanked and I lost *everything* with almost a hundred thousand dollars in debt. To say I was stressed back then is an understatement.

Shortly after that, I came back home to Dallas, Texas, to start over. I recovered somewhat – I started eating better, working out, meditating a little bit – but I felt like I was a failure. My business had failed. I blamed myself. I quickly went back to being a "corporate zombie," working in learning and development in high tech for the next few years. I was still stressed, unhappy, taking anti-depressants and anti-anxiety meds, and was back in counseling with no real improvement.

By 2008, I worked for a giant telecom in Dallas, and I was completely miserable, working for a rigid, demanding boss, doing work that was completely unfulfilling. I was an entrepreneur at heart and wanted to be doing something that would help "change the world." I had always been interested in alternative health and healing, so I started to google "energy healing schools." I discovered the Lionheart Institute in San Antonio, Texas. I could drive there, and it was led and taught by former teachers and deans of Barbara Brennan's Healing Science School, which I had always wanted to attend but it had not been feasible as it was a full-time school in New York. I was super excited!

During my three-year intense program at Lionheart, I learned something that changed my life forever – characterology. Characterology is the study of the five character structures or types, originated by Austrian psychoanalyst Wilhelm Reich in the 1930s. Characterology completely changed my perspective on life and everyone around me. Finally, everything about myself and everyone I knew made complete sense.

The five character types are sets of patterns formed in response to trauma at different stages of development, starting in utero up to seven or eight years of age. Each type forms at a different stage of development. These patterns are defense strategies or tendencies that influence body shape, physical and personality traits, beliefs, thoughts, emotions, behaviors, talents, gifts, issues, and challenges. I finally understood why I had such a hard time losing weight, why I overworked, and why I had a hard time standing up for myself, being in the spotlight, and so on.

This fascinated me more than anything I had ever learned. During my study of characterology, I went through the most intense healing I had ever gone through. It was like the "dark night of the soul," as we had to heal all of our types in the course. It was very challenging, and quite a few people dropped out because they were not ready to truly face their demons.

I had been in traditional counseling (talk therapy) for well over a decade, and it had not made that much of a difference. But characterology? All the difference in the world. I was a completely different person. I lost weight, started seeing an amazing man, started having fun again, dressing differently, and dipping my foot into things like standup comedy. I was completely comfortable in my own skin, something I had not been in a long time. My regular psychotherapist got upset with me and started criticizing both me and Lionheart, so I fired her! Lionheart had taught me that somatic or body-based therapies (like characterology and bioenergetics) were at least ten times more effective than any counseling I had had before. I was not about go backward!

Once I graduated from Lionheart, I started my mind-body practice. I even got my teacher training certification and co-taught several trainings. In my practice, I did hands-on energy work, as well as coaching and counseling. When I used characterology on my clients, it seemed to work so well. Every one of them was fascinated by how much I seemed to know about them during our first meetings. All of a sudden, I had X-ray vision for just about everyone I met. I could look at someone and know a hundred things about them because I had learned characterology. It was cool (but also a bit unnerving) to have this knowledge. My clients would ask me, "Where can I find out more about this?" or, "Is there a book on this?" At the time, there were only large tomes that were written for therapists or healers, but nothing for the average person. I said to myself back then, "I need to write a book on this."

I continued on this path as a mind-body coach and practitioner, mainly helping people in physical, emotional or professional crisis, while still keeping my day job at a global software company. I was still afraid to really go out on my own. Outside of my business in California, my entire professional career had been in corporate learning and development, mainly designing and leading large corporate learning programs, both in-person and online. I was scared to go outside my comfort zone. So I stayed put, playing it safe. At this point, I was back in full corporate zombie mode and was overworked, exhausted, unmotivated, and overweight, with many health problems. I know what you are thinking, *why* wasn't I practicing all of the amazing stuff I had learned before? Why wasn't I practicing what I was helping my clients with? Real change is hard and my patterns were very strong and very deep. Basically, the corporate world was a replacement for my demanding father, who I so wanted to please.

During this time, I was working with a personal trainer in Dallas who kept telling me, "Until you live a life of passion, nothing is going to change much." He was right. At this point, I knew I needed to write a book and design and run a program having to do with characterology. But how? I couldn't just quit my job and do it. And this stuff is a bit complicated. But if anyone could do it, I could. I am a writer with a degree in journalism, a learning program designer, and a former business owner and entrepreneur. But how would I make this consumable for the average person? It was a bit daunting, so I put it to the side, as usual.

Then I decided to move to New York City with the same job, but my health was continuing to suffer. I was back in full corporate-zombie mode and so unhappy and overworked in my corporate job. I was completely burned out and could barely function. When I went to see a functional medicine specialist to get "my energy up," I will never forget what he said as he walked through the door with my test results:

He said, "So how long have you been dealing with toxic stress?"

I said, "Um, my whole life."

He said, "Looks like it."

I asked him how he knew and he said, "Your cortisol."

"But you didn't test for that?"

He said, "I didn't need to because it didn't show up in your blood at all. And when it is not in your blood, it is not in your body. Which means your body has not been producing it for years. I am actually surprised you are still alive walking around and functioning."

I was stage 4 adrenal exhaustion where your adrenals stop working. It even had the skull and crossbones on the chart. My doctor said it would take a minimum of two years to heal. That was a major wakeup call for me. I knew I had to do something different or I was going to die. I changed my diet and my sleep patterns, worked less hours, and took supplements. I got a little better but was still very unhappy and zombie-like.

Meanwhile, I decided to take a program that changed my life – Mama Gena's School of Womanly Arts. It focused a lot on tuning into your desires and how much power there is in your desires. It also included a lot of emotional embodiment work. It reinforced the anger work I had learned and practiced those many years ago – about how powerful it was to get those bottled up emotions *out* of your body... especially for me and my character type. I started practicing the anger work again. It was still a bit tricky because I had a dog and lived in an apartment building, but I did it occasionally. A few of us would rent out audition rooms in Manhattan to practice in as a group since they were soundproof and we could go "full out" in there. It was amazing!

At that point, I knew I needed to change what I was doing for my work. I needed to live my passion; I could no longer be the corporate zombie. So I moved back to Texas, took a few months off work, and I practiced the desire work and the anger work. My whole life changed quickly and dramatically. I got retested and there was no sign of adrenal exhaustion. I was cured in less than six months. I was back in the flow of my life and things just started happening very quickly for me. Using characterology, I wrote my first book, *Come Alive*, and developed the companion program. I modified and renamed the character types to be more consumable to the public. I focused on helping undervalued professional women who had never really found their passion or lived it. I quit my corporate job. Immediately afterward, clients and money started flowing to me. It was just so easy once I was in the flow and made the decision, based solely on my true passion.

While I was leading the Come Alive program, I noticed that most of my clients wanted to really "hang out" in the "tackling challenges" stage of the Come Alive process. That is the part where we do the emotional embodiment work in which you get what is on the inside *out* of your head and your body. I extended my program a few weeks because there was so much work to be done in that stage.

Additionally, when I would go to events or speaking engagements, I would get approached by mostly men and entrepreneurs or leaders who were fascinated by the character types and my work, asking if I could help them too. So I did. The thing that they needed help on the most was something I was *very* familiar with: handling chronic stress.

Then I went back to my characterology notes and looked at each type and realized that the emotional patterns and energy patterns of each type directly related to how that type handled stress, that is, that your character type defines your stress triggers, your energetic pattern or reaction to those triggers (fight, flight, freeze, hold, hide), and your emotional and behavioral reactions to those triggers. When I connected those dots, it was like a *poof*...it all fit together so well, and I knew I needed to write another book and program, taking a deep dive into conquering stress using characterology.

So I updated the character types since each type describes not only how you handle stress, but also what kind of leader or entrepreneur you are. I added the many practices that I had learned and developed over the years, and I created the Lose-It method for defeating stress. The key to defeating chronic stress is getting what is on the inside *out* of your head and your body so that you can be the leader you were meant to be. To "lose" all of the sh*t that does not serve you.

I have spent years trying to figure this all out. Now that I have, I want to shout it from the rooftops! I want to share it with everyone on the planet. But for now, I am sharing it with you.

It certainly won't take you the 20 years that it took me to get to this place because I am here to guide you every step of the way. I have taken my journey and experience and created a simple process for you to follow. No matter where you are in your stress-defeating journey, you will get something out of this book. Whether you are just a reader or a participant in the Lose-It program, this book is meant to be read, worked through, and used as a reference over and over. Shall we begin?

CHAPTER 3: THE LOSE-IT METHOD

*"It's not the load that breaks you down,
it's the way you carry it."*

– Lou Holt

The Lose-It Method came together when I was working with clients on my Come Alive program that helps people find and live their passion. There was a piece of that process I called "The Inside Out," which helped them dig down deep to get what was on the inside out of their head and their body. This part of the process became the part where everyone wanted "to stay in" for a while because there was a lot of work to be done. They all kept telling me, "This is the gold. This should be your program." That part really changed all aspects of their lives. They also noted how much their daily stress had reduced.

After getting approached by entrepreneurs to help them with the constant pressure they were under, I decided to dive in deeper and pull out that part of my original process and expound on it to create the Lose-It Method.

Once I made the connection that the emotional patterns and energy patterns of each type directly related to how that type handled stress, it was so easy. Defeating stress is using the mind and the body. The stress itself is not the problem – it is how we react to it. And our reactions are mostly based on our patterns, our "programming," and the "stories in our head." If we can repair those patterns, create new patterns, and rewrite our "programs" and stories, we can defeat it. I am living proof!

This method is a unique process, unlike any you will have experienced. It is challenging, deep, and life-altering. It has helped many people overcome their challenges and their chronic stress to become the leaders they always knew they could be.

Here is an overview of the method, which I will cover step by step in the next several chapters.

The Lose-It Method

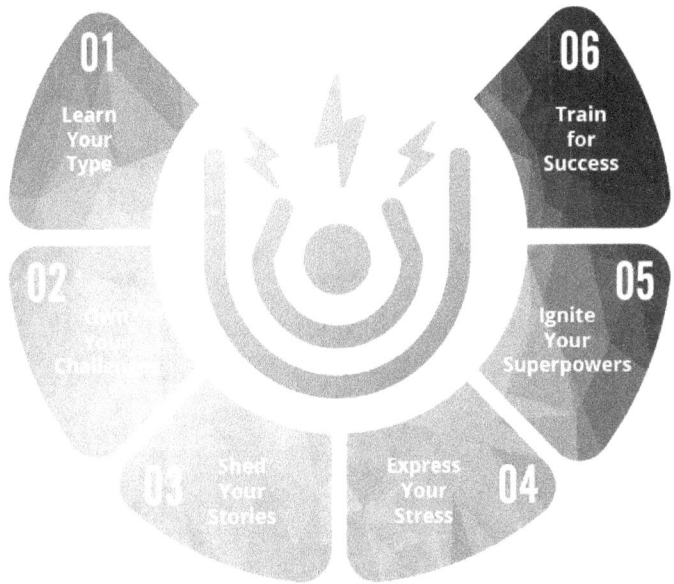

1.   L – Learn Your Type

We start off by identifying your Character Type, which helps you understand what type of leader you are, how you handle stress, and why. This includes a quiz.

2.   O – Own Your Challenges

After learning more about your type, you can easily identify your stress triggers, patterns and your reactions or defenses to those triggers. Write them down and *own* them.

3.   S – Shed Your Stories

Much of the time when a stress response gets triggered, it comes from the "sh*t stories in your head," based on some memory of an event from your past. This is where you will identify those stories and write them down to get them *out* of your head. Then document any recurring or limiting beliefs you notice and let them go. You will create your own inner supervillain to support you in this step.

4.   E – Express Your Stress

Knowing the source of your stories and limiting beliefs really helps you connect the dots and may bring your stress and your emotions to the surface. In this step, you will learn how to effectively release your stress by fully expressing your stress and your emotions and clearing them *out* of your head and your body.

5.   I – Ignite Your Superpowers

It is amazing what happens after release – your whole world changes and all your true genius comes to the surface. In this step, you will identify the "superpowers" that you want to own as a leader moving forward. You will create your own inner superhero to support you in this step.

6.   T – Train for Success

The final step is to create your intention and an accountability plan of how you will measure success and regularly use the practices in this program to ensure your continued emotional fitness as a true leader in your company, industry, and the world!

How to Get the Most Out of This Book

Journal and Pens

I suggest you use or get a notebook or journal to use throughout this process. You will use it to take notes, write down your stories, write down answers to your inquiries, and do some of the activities throughout the process. You can always use your computer or tablet to take notes, but I find it really helpful to physically write out your notes, stories and ideas. And if you are creative and like to draw or doodle, get some cool, colored pens or pencils.

Partner

This book and process can be challenging for a lot of people. You may need a support system. If you're not participating in the Lose-It program, you may want to find a partner or even a group to go through this with you. I think it is important to be supported as you go through the process as it helps you to be accountable through your own journey. You may also want to take a picture of yourself at the beginning of this journey and share it with your partner or group. Then take another one at the end and compare the two. See how you have changed. You may lose weight (if you need to), you may look younger (defeating stress does that to you!), or you may just have a sparkle in your eyes that was not there before. Anything is possible!

Self-Care Practices

I believe that in a journey to conquering stress, it is vital to have self-care practices. And I know that entrepreneurs are the *worst* at self-care. What do I mean by self-care? I mean regular practices to help regulate and calm your body. That may include things like a grounding meditation, get1ting a massage, going for a walk outside, doing yoga, Tai Chi, Qi Gong, etc. I suggest you create a self-care practice inventory in your journal, making note of the practices that resonate with you and that you can do on a regular basis. You can also create this inventory in a spreadsheet or another app on your phone or computer. Whatever works for you. Mine is organized by the following categories:

- Personal self-care (like meditation, taking a nap, hot bath, journaling, etc.)

- Partner activities (activities in which I need a partner– like roleplays or other activities that you will learn in this book)

- Movement and sports (like hiking in nature, cycling, swimming)

- Therapies (suggested therapies or practices in which I need a practitioner – like massage, chiropractor, energy work, acupuncture)

I have included some practices throughout this book, but here is one that you can do on a regular basis. I share this here because it is a great one to do first thing in the morning, every morning. It really helps ground and calm you and prepare you for the day.

Activity – The Three-Body Check-In (Time required 10–15 minutes)

I am a big proponent of meditation. The quality of my life is directly tied to how often I meditate. I find that meditation helped me tremendously as an entrepreneur, especially when I was practicing it every morning or every evening. I have a few different types of meditation I do regularly, but the one I do most regularly is the three-body check-in. When I was studying at Lionheart, I learned that we have three different "bodies" – the physical body, the emotional body, and the mental body. These three "bodies" regulate your system. No matter what is going on with me, this check-in really helps calm and clear my body, emotions, and mind for the day. It helps ground me and keep me fully present. This check-in is a combination meditation and writing exercise and goes something like this:

1. Sit comfortably in a chair with your back straight, feet on the floor, and a pen and paper or journal close by. You may want to use headphones to listen to meditative music.

2. Close your eyes and notice your breath. If it is shallow, try to deepen it. If it is fast, try to slow it down. Do this until you feel your breath start to regulate (that is, when your inhale and exhale match for a count of 3-4).

3. Then start the check-in with your physical body. Begin with your feet and do a slow upward scan of your body, noticing anything that is off or needs

attention. Write down any sensations or anything of concern. Once done, thank your physical body for serving you today.

4. Move on to your emotions, or the emotional body. Again, notice your breath and regulate it as best you can. With eyes closed, ask yourself how you are feeling emotionally. Are you sad, angry, frustrated, joyful? Write down whatever emotions are present for you. You can write something like, "Today, I am feeling _____." Once done, thank your emotions for serving and protecting you today.

5. Move on to the mind, or the mental body. Once more, notice your breath and regulate it as best you can. Ask yourself, "What recurring thoughts or beliefs are popping up today?" Write them down. Once done, thank your mind and your beliefs for serving and protecting you today.

6. End with an overall gratitude to all three. Write down at least one thing you are grateful for today.

Okay, it is time to begin the process. Are you ready? The next chapter is the first step: Learn Your Character Type.

CHAPTER 4: STEP 1 – LEARN YOUR TYPE

"It's not the stress that kills us, it is our reaction to it."

– Hans Selye

The Five Character Types

What are the Five Character Types? A little background first... In my work as a mind-body practitioner, I studied the five character structures created by Austrian psychoanalyst Wilhelm Reich in the 1930s. As I said in chapter 2, the five character structures or *types* are sets of patterns formed in response to trauma at different stages of development, starting in utero up to six or seven years of age. And by trauma, I mean anything that caused distress to you at that young age. We have all suffered trauma. That does not mean that you had a "bad childhood" or "bad parents." It could mean that, but it simply means you are human. These patterns that formed in the stages are defense strategies or tendencies that influence body shape, physical and personality traits, beliefs, thoughts, emotions, behaviors, talents, gifts, issues, and challenges.

Over the years, many people have taken Reich's work and modified it in different ways (see Further Reading in the back of book for more information). I have modified and simplified his work so that it can easily be used for personal development, leadership development and stress management. They will help you discover what kind of entrepreneur or leader you naturally are, how you handle stress and why. It is important to note that you may have more than one dominant type. We all have a little of all of them. But usually, one to two of them are more dominant.

I will go into a description of each type first so you get the idea. Then at the end of the chapter is an assessment in the form of a checklist that you can complete and see where you stand. This step can make you a bit uncomfortable. I know when I first learned about the types, it was hard to acknowledge that I had some of these traits, especially the negative ones. But once I took it all in, I took this big sigh of relief and said, "Oh, that's why I do that" and "No wonder that has been so hard for me most of my life." It gave me such a sense of freedom and really helped me to stop blaming or shaming myself for reacting a certain way. I hope it does for you as well. Keep in mind that we will go more into the challenges and stress triggers in the next chapter.

A little note about the physical traits associated with each type. You do not have to have the physical traits of that type in order for it to be considered a dominant type, but if you *do* possess the physical traits, then you are *definitely* that type. And the more work you do on yourself, the more the negative traits will diminish, including the physical ones.

Remember that you do not have to have every quality to be that type and you may be more than one type. I myself am a combination. Just notice what resonates with you. Or maybe you know someone who fits one or more of the types. Like, "Oh, wow, that is why my spouse or my business partner is like this or does that." It's very informative and helps you understand not only yourself but everyone around you. Okay, let's dive into the Five Types!

The Dreamer

The first type is the Dreamer. The Dreamer suffered trauma or some kind of distress from in utero to six months old. The Dreamer either suffered trauma in the womb or during birth or did not get the attention needed at that very early stage.

If you are a Dreamer, you have almost always been very thin with large eyes. You are *the creative genius* of your company or organization, the one who comes up with the brilliant ideas, comes up with innovative solutions to big problems. You are highly intellectual and may be gifted artistically or into math or science. The nerd. You're more comfortable connecting through devices than in person. You are highly independent and prefer to work and live alone. That is how you get your power: from being alone. The innovator or inventor type. The mad scientist. You live in your head most of the time and are not good with intimate relationships or partnerships. You may be great at coming up with the idea for a business but not-so-great at actually running the day-to-day affairs. You have a tendency to undercharge for your services. You have issues connecting one-on-one with others and can suffer from social anxiety. You may even be considered socially awkward. There is a deep hidden fear inside that has always been there.

The Dreamer's stress pattern is freeze or flight and breathing is arrested or shallow. You may be triggered by being around too many people, social interaction, or being the center of attention. You may have a hard time looking people in the eyes or holding that contact. Your energy leaves your body when you are triggered.

You may react to stress with extreme anxiety, worry, nervousness, panic, ruminating thoughts, losing things, falling down or running into things, fast talking, disappearing on or "ghosting" people, forgetfulness, distraction or lack of focus. You may even have a tendency toward medication or substances to handle your extreme anxiety. Dreamers can also suffer from PTSD.

Think Steve Jobs, Mark Zuckerberg, Prince, Michael Jackson, Tina Fey, Benedict Cumberbatch's *Sherlock*, or Sheldon from The *Big Bang Theory*. Those are all Dreamers.

The Charmer

The second type is the Charmer. The Charmer suffered trauma or some kind of distress from six months to two years old, most likely from not getting enough nourishment, time, or attention at this stage, and as an adult feeling like nothing is ever enough.

If you are a Charmer, your upper body (mainly shoulders, rib cage) is usually smaller and weaker than your lower body or was when you were an adolescent. It can be hard to tell on men as that can be seen as a sign of weakness, so men will most likely bulk out the upper body with weights in order to compensate.

The Charmer is a gifted communicator and loves to be the center of attention. You are the performer, *the star* of your company or organization. You cannot get enough attention. You need fans. You are charming and persuasive and love to sell. You can sell anything to anybody. You have a need to "talk things out" with someone; you have a need to be heard. You are a natural teacher and love to share information. You bond easily with others and make a great collaborator. You are very skilled at marketing and work extremely well with the public. You love to ask others for their opinions or advice. You post on social media a lot. You are really good at getting what you want and you can even get others to do your work for you. I mean, what's wrong with that? It just gives you more time for you to bask in the limelight!

But in some Charmers, there is this deep sense of loss inside that nothing seems to satisfy. There is never enough money, love, or attention. You are always seeking more of … everything. You may have had addiction problems (food, cigarettes, substances, shopping, etc.) to fill that unfillable need. You use your sexual energy to get what you want. You love to flirt and to be served. You can go back and forth from being extremely generous and giving to appearing very greedy. You are usually very dependent on others both at home and at work; you do not like to be alone. That is how you get your power, from being with others, plugging into their energy. Being alone or feeling abandoned triggers you *big time* and your energy pattern is to go out to others and then pull that energy back in.

Your reaction to stress is to sometimes lash out at others for perceived abandonment or rejection or from someone taking something away from you, and then trying to draw or pull them back in. A bit of manipulation. You like playing the victim and may get emotional when things do not go your way. Pouting is a hobby of yours. You may withhold affection or attention to "punish" someone who did not give you what you wanted, when you wanted it. You may even be known to throw "adult temper tantrums." If you have ever been called "a drama queen or king," you are definitely a Charmer. A lot of celebrities or "influencers" are Charmers.

Think Kim Kardashian, Beyoncé, Lady Gaga, Mick Jagger, Jennifer Lopez, Jeff Bezos, and Oprah Winfrey. Those are all Charmers.

The Endurer

The third type is the Endurer. The Endurer suffered trauma or some kind of distress from two to three years old, most likely from not being allowed to fully express yourself – it was not safe to be your full, true self.

If you are an Endurer, you have almost always had a weight problem (like 30 or more pounds overweight) because you learned to hold *everything* inside. And the excess weight can even be muscle – some men may bulk out with weights to create that boundary. You are *the industrious leader*, the tireless one, the workhorse with a tendency to carry the load for your company. You are a kind and compassionate leader and have a tendency to rescue others. You are sensitive to the feelings of others and are always thinking of others first, like your employees or family. You will fight like hell to protect your team or employees. You put yourself last, always. You get your power from being of service to others.

You are extremely capable and can do the work of many people and have a tendency to overwork, even to the point of collapse. You put your own health at risk to please others and to be "a team player." You are terrible at delegating. You are not good at setting boundaries with others. You volunteer to stay late and do other's work, all the while resenting them for it. You always put on a good face, but deep down inside, there is a boiling rage. It may come out sideways sometimes because you've held it in for so long. Sometimes, you even enjoy complaining or being the victim or martyr in situations. You may say to yourself, "When is it going to be *my* turn for success and happiness?" You are a people pleaser. You are very uncomfortable talking about your feelings, standing up for yourself, and bringing uncomfortable topics up to forefront. You would just prefer to suffer in silence rather than offend anyone. Your inner critic is very strong; your negative self-talk happens frequently. You engage in self-deprecating humor to mask what is going on inside.

The Endurer's energy pattern is to hide – that is, holding back, inside and down, like compressed energy. You may be triggered by criticism of any kind, someone bullying or taking advantage of someone on your team or in your family, someone violating a boundary, or the success of someone else (sparks envy). You don't like the spotlight and if the light is shown on you, you get very triggered because you were never allowed to show your real self so it creates a huge conflict because you want to show it SO badly but you are terrified to do so.

You react to stress with holding everything in, complaining, passive aggressive behavior, holding a grudge, or perhaps lashing out at someone who criticizes you; once you cannot hold it in any longer, you have an outburst. This is the type that feels the most amount of stress because you learned not to let it out at an early age. That it was dangerous for you to do so. You did not fully learn to process your emotions, especially anger. This pattern is very strong and hard to break. But it is possible (I am living proof!).

Think Marc Benioff from Salesforce, Oprah Winfrey (combination Charmer Endurer), Donald Trump, John Goodman, Kevin James, Samwise from *Lord of the Rings*, Hagrid from *Harry Potter*, Popeye, Eeyore from *Winnie the Pooh*, and my all-time favorite Endurer, The Hulk from Marvel. Those are all Endurers.

The Commander

The fourth type is the Commander. The Commander suffered trauma or some kind of distress from three to five years old – most likely a betrayal of the heart caused by being favored by one parent but only for a limited amount of time. Commanders never really learned to fully trust someone.

If you are a Commander, your upper body is most likely larger than your lower body (like an inflated chest, broad shoulders, narrow hips). You are the fearless leader. You are visionary, confident, passionate, courageous, and not afraid to take risks. You are adventurous, loyal, and protective of your employees. You have the ability to go, go, go and make things happen. You encourage others to be the best they can be. You like to be the one in charge, in everything you do. You do not like it when you are not in charge. You like giving orders. Why wouldn't you? You're really good at it! Being seen as successful is very important

35

to you. You get your power from being in control and leading others. You are very comfortable speaking to large crowds. You love being the smartest person in the room. In fact if you are not, you get triggered. You cannot stand being wrong, you must win every argument, and you will go to lengths to prove you are right, *even* when you know you are wrong. If someone on your team challenges you, you do not react well. You consider it a betrayal and may even lash out at or punish them in some way. Sometimes you see betrayal and disloyalty in the smallest of actions in others. You may think of yourself as special and even above others. You may even have a tendency toward narcissism.

The Commander's energy or stress holding pattern is *energy* out, projecting out, dominating others. It is like the fight in fight-or-flight. You are triggered by *not* being in control, being wrong, someone shining a light on one of your flaws, criticism (no matter how tiny), calling you out on something or blaming you for something, even if you were responsible. You may react by lashing out at others (directly or indirectly), losing control, being very aggressive and even attacking, having an outburst or blowing up at people (short fuse), or barking orders at people. You may avoid/bad-mouth/seek revenge on those who have called you out on something, like a punishment. You may even be known for being a "hot head" or encouraged to seek help for anger management or outbursts.

Think Elon Musk, The Rock, Donald Trump (combination Endurer Commander), Kanye West, Madonna, Thor from Marvel, Buzz Lightyear from *Toy Story*, Mr. Incredible, and Indiana Jones from *Raiders of the*

Lost Ark. Also, almost any professional U.S. football player. Those are all Commanders.

The Achiever

The fifth and final type is the Achiever. The Achiever suffered trauma or some kind of distress from five to eight years old – most likely a rejection from a parent of what was considered "incorrect" behavior, creating a rejection and loss of your authenticity or true sense of self.

If you are an Achiever, you have almost always been lean, fit, and well proportioned. You have incredible integrity, clarity, and balance. You are *the virtuous leader.* Your moral compass is strong. You are determined, ambitious, and competitive. You do not like to lose. You appreciate and demand beauty, quality, and perfection in everything that you do, and you demand that of your employees or team. You have never missed a deadline. You make sure your team knows exactly what to do and by when. And you are sure to treat *all* of your employees fairly. You do not tolerate unfairness or injustice well.

You are always dressed appropriately and immaculately. You are most likely athletic and/or a high-achiever. Your home, office, and desk are always clean and perfectly organized. You are very organized and love having plans. Spontaneity is not your friend. If things are not perfect, you get anxious. You will work tirelessly for perfection. You are not good with emotions. Showing emotions is a sign of weakness. You may not even know you have emotions sometimes. Being truly authentic and vulnerable is very difficult for you because then you wouldn't be perfect! You avoid being vulnerable at all costs. People may even describe you as cold, aloof, or superficial at times. You're not, but that is how you may appear to others.

The Achiever's energy or stress-holding pattern is complete containment and holding back. It is similar to hiding in the Endurer but it is more evenly held throughout the body. You hold your body in so tight that you may have spinal issues as a result. Nothing is getting in or out. You are triggered by you *not* being perfect or not winning, by things around you not being perfect, not on time, or not according to your plan. A missed deadline will definitely trigger you. You are also triggered by messiness or chaos of any kind. It makes you highly anxious. But you usually do not react in any outward kind of way, toward others. You may react by exercising obsessively, cleaning obsessively, or busying yourself with "getting things done." *Anything* not to feel the anxiety or emotions that may start to rise up. You have to be busy and productive at all times. Constant achievement is a goal. It is very hard for you to just sit, relax, and do nothing. It is common for the Achiever to be in combination with the Dreamer.

Think Steve Jobs (combination Dreamer Achiever), Barack Obama, Nicole Kidman, Jerry Seinfeld, Monica from *Friends*, Hermione from *Harry Potter*. Those are all Achievers.

The 5 Character Type Assessment

Now that you have an overview for each type, you may recognize some traits in yourself. It is time to take the quiz to be sure. Review the groupings of statements below and put a check by each one that is true for you. Then add up how many checks you have in each section. The ones with the most checks will be your dominant type(s). Most people have one to two dominant types. Some of these statements may sound odd, but they help determine your type. Just go with it! Please be completely honest. This is *only* for you to see (no one else). If you do not feel like you're sure about your type, you may consider taking the full assessment on our website here: comealiveinstitute.com.

The Dreamer – The Creative Genius

1. ___ I love spending time alone.

2. ___ For most of my life, I have been thin and have had a hard time gaining weight.

3. ___ I have a problem with anxiety or worry.

4. ___ I am fiercely independent and prefer working alone.

5. ___ I am easily distracted and have a hard time focusing on one thing for long.

6. ___ I am uncomfortable or a bit awkward in social situations.

7. ___ I love animals and often prefer being with them more than people.

8. ___ I love spending time in nature and would rather be there than with people.

9. ___ I am gifted artistically (music, singing, performing, fine art, etc.)

10. ___ I am intellectual and nerdy and am more comfortable interacting with people through devices (phone, tablet, computer) than in person.

11. ___ I am a creative visionary and the "idea person" at my company but have a hard time executing or seeing things through to fruition.

12. ___ I am innovative problem-solver – I come up with innovative solutions to big problems.

13. ___ I do not make the kind of money I should (don't charge enough for services, do not get paid for my real talents, etc.).

14. ___ I am in my head a lot and sometimes have a hard time connecting with others.

15. ___ Being in a relationship is not that important to me.

16. ___ I am very uncomfortable being the center of attention.

Total _____

The Charmer – The Star

17. ___ I do not enjoy being alone.

18. ___ I have almost always been in a long-term relationship (rarely without a partner).

19. ___ My upper body is smaller than my lower body (shoulders narrower than hips) or was when I was an adolescent.

20. ___ It is important for me to be heard and "talk things out" with my partner, colleague or employee, or even on social media.

21. ___ I have a gift with words, both writing and speaking.

22. ___ I love selling and marketing.

23. ___ I am very generous and love giving gifts for others.

24. ___ I love to share information and teach others.

25. ___ I am very persuasive; I can easily get others to do what I want them to do.

26. ___ I prefer collaboration and working with others rather than working alone.

27. ___ Sometimes I feel like my needs are never going to be met.

28. ___ Most of the time, I never feel like I have enough (money, love, power, affection, etc.).

29. ___ I need validation from others (boss, colleague, partner, employees, family).

30. ___ I enjoy being the center of attention and like to perform for others.

31. ___ I can take things personally and get hurt easily.

32. ___ I have (or have had) issues with addictions (cigarettes, alcohol, substances, food, shopping or sex).

Total ___

The Endurer – The Industrious Leader

33. ___ I have or have had weight problems in my life (thirty-plus pounds overweight).

34. ___ I have tendency to over-give, both at home and at work.

35. ___ I am hard working and responsible and can do the work of many people.

36. ___ I do not delegate well and have a tendency to rescue others.

37. ___ I am a kind and compassionate leader and really know how to take care of my team.

38. ___ Sometimes I am afraid to show the "real me" as others may not like or accept me.

39. ___ I will sacrifice (time, relationships, my health, etc.) for my business.

40. ___ I am very generous with my time and attention.

41. ___ I appear cool, calm and collected on the outside, while inside I may be boiling.

42. ___ I have a tendency to hold grudges when someone has wronged me.

43. ___ I do not speak up for myself like I should and have hard time saying "no" and setting boundaries with others (partners, family, at work, etc.).

44. ___ Sometimes I am afraid if I really let my anger out, I could hurt myself or someone else – better to just let it stay inside.

45. ___ I sometimes resent others who are successful and seem to have it "so easy" and ask myself, "When is it going to be *my* turn?"

46. ___ I feel like it is more important to please others than fulfill my own needs.

47. ___ I am very sensitive and am crushed by criticism.

48. ___ I do not like attention on myself and have a hard time being seen and "putting myself out there."

Total ___

The Commander – The Fearless Leader

49. ___ I am a great leader.

50. ___ My upper body is larger than my lower body (chest/shoulders wider than hips)

51. ___ I am very confident in my abilities.

52. ___ I am visionary and entrepreneurial.

53. ___ I am a "take charge" kind of person. I make things happen.

54. ___ I do not like being wrong and will go to lengths to prove "I am right."

55. ___ I like to lead every project or endeavor I am a part of and have a hard time letting someone else lead.

56. ___ I am brave, spontaneous, and willing to take risks.

57. ___ I have the ability to manifest my vision and dreams and inspire others to do the same.

58. ___ I am comfortable on a stage, speaking in front of crowds.

59. ___ I am very generous to those who are loyal to me.

60. ___ I have a hard time apologizing (even when I know I am wrong).

61. ___ I like to be the "smartest person in the room."

62. ___ I like giving orders and being in control of situations.

63. ___ I hate to admit this, but when someone crosses me, I want to retaliate in some way.

64. ___ I am afraid to show weakness or be vulnerable in front of others.

Total ____

The Achiever – The Virtuous Leader

65. ___ I have never had a weight problem and my body is well-proportioned.

66. ___ Appearances are very important to me.

67. ___ I aim for perfection in everything that I do and expect that in my team.

68. ___ I have very healthy boundaries and do not have problem saying *no* to others.

69. ___ I am fair and balanced and try to operate from integrity at all times.

70. ___ I have a fear of losing control so I keep my emotions in check at all times.

71. ___ I have a hard time being spontaneous and do not like to change plans.

72. ___ My home, workspace, and desk are always neat and put together.

73. ___ I am highly competitive and do not like to surrender in any way.

74. ___ I have rarely, if ever, missed a deadline.

75. ___ I am a high-achiever and take pride in my accomplishments.

76. ___ I am ambitious and driven and make a good, fair leader.

77. ___ I am afraid of my feelings sometimes so I just push them down.

78. ___ People have told me that I can seem cold and unfeeling.

79. ___ I have a hard time being vulnerable.

80. ___ I have a hard time showing my real self, instead of who I am "supposed to be."

Total ___

The Results

The 5 types are listed below. Write down the total for each one:

1. The Dreamer ___
2. The Charmer ___
3. The Endurer ___
4. The Commander ___
5. The Achiever ___

So, which type had the most checks? If you got over 10 checks for any type, that will most likely be a dominant type. Are you a combination of two or more types? I am a combination of myself (Dreamer, Endurer, and Commander). You may want to take some notes in your journal about your dominant type(s) as that will be helpful moving forward.

Knowing your type is a really important first step to conquering your stress as it helps you to become aware of what triggers your own stress response, why, and your reaction to it. That alone can help reduce your stress somewhat. And learning about the types also helps you understand others in your life and that can help reduce stress as well.

Let's move on to the next chapter to *Own Your Challenges* and go into more detail about the types as well as your triggers, patterns and defenses.

LOSE YOUR SH*T

CHAPTER 5: STEP 2 – OWN YOUR CHALLENGES

*"Somehow our devils are never quite what we
expect when we meet them face to face."*
– Nelson DeMille

Now that you have identified and learned more about your Character Type, let's dive into identifying your current challenges, that is what is causing pressure in your life, your stresses. Take out your journal and write down what you think is currently challenging you in your business and your personal life. These can be anything: for example, I am worried about making payroll, I am worried that my business will not succeed, the economy is tanking, my ex is driving me crazy, there is not enough time to get everything done I need to get done, I don't spend enough time with my kids, I wish I had more time to just chill, and so on.

Most of the time, the things that we think cause us worry and stress are things that are outside of our control, but in reality most of our stress "happens" because we are "programmed" to react a certain way to certain triggers based on the patterns from our past. It is these little events or triggers that happen throughout your day – that you react to and don't even know that they are happening because it is your programming – that wreak havoc in your head and in your body.

In my experience, when you can identify or recognize those patterns – that is, what triggers you and how you react to it – and connect some of the dots, it is half the battle in defeating your stress. Your reactions include bodily reactions (how your energy reacts), as well as emotional and behavioral reactions. Once you recognize and start to own them, you become aware of when they happen and you may be able to alter them or go in a different direction. But for now, awareness is the key.

Now let's do an exercise to help bring more awareness to your own patterns. Listed below for each type are:

- Common triggers – these are underlying causes of your stress, what presses your buttons, sets you off, or makes you uncomfortable
- Energy/stress patterns – what your energy/body does when you're triggered
- Common defenses – emotional reactions and behaviors when you're triggered

Review them and highlight what is true for you. Be honest. This is not about shaming you, but looking at the truth so you can perhaps change the undesired patterns which will drastically reduce your stress in the long run. Then take out your journal or notebook and write down your most common triggers, your energy/stress patterns and your defenses and reactions. And add any additional ones that may not be listed here. And then really look at them. You may even want to tell them to your partner or trusted friend. Post them on your wall. And then over the next few days, try to make a checkmark next to the ones you notice happening and how frequently they happen. Again, this is just bringing this into your awareness for you. In the next chapter, we will go further.

The Dreamer – Triggers, Patterns, Defenses

Common Triggers (For Your Stress)

- Too much social interaction
- Being the center of attention
- Working with others (instead of alone)
- Being called out or called on to present in public
- Playing team sports
- Loud noises or someone being aggressive toward you or in your presence
- Getting too close to others (intimate connections)

Energy Stress Patterns (When Triggered)

- Freeze (from fear) – energy stops and full body tension starts
- Flight or withdrawal – energy goes up and out of body (disappears)

Common Emotional Reactions and Defensive Behaviors

- Main emotion when triggered: fear
- Anxiety and worry, panic
- Hypervigilance, insomnia
- Spacing out, daydreaming, overwhelmed, distracted behavior, procrastination
- Doesn't follow through or finish projects through to the end

- Forgetfulness, losing things, getting lost easily (not good with directions, maps)
- Freezing, being quiet/not speaking up, disappearing/"ghosting," isolation
- Intellectualization, showing intellectual superiority
- Hurried behavior/speech, spurts of energy, followed by exhaustion
- Disorganization, messiness, losing things, tripping or falling down
- Obsessive thoughts, rumination, paranoia
- Panic, "freaking out," possible suicidal thoughts
- Possible addictions or escape mechanisms – alcohol or anti-anxiety medication to feel "normal" or to be able to connect to others, sleep meds for insomnia, possible opioid addiction for intense anxiety/pain, playing computer games (device addiction)

The Charmer – Triggers, Patterns, Defenses

Common Triggers (For Your Stress)

- Being alone
- Rejection or perceived rejection or abandonment
- Something being withdrawn or taken away (love, money, job, affection, funding)
- Losing a client or business
- Not getting your way

- Not getting enough attention or validation from others

Energy Stress Patterns (When Triggered)

- Pulling in/sucking in– energy going out and then pulling back in from others
- Withdrawing – sometimes as punishment to perceived rejection

Common Emotional Reactions and Defensive Behaviors

- Main emotion when triggered: hurt
- Communicates with emotions, very emotional, can fall apart easily
- Neediness, victimization ("poor me"), whininess, co-dependence
- Makes demands of others, expects others to take care of your needs (without expressing those needs)
- Extreme feelings of unworthiness
- Drama – acting out to get attention, overreacting to perceived rejection
- Manipulation, blaming others for problems
- Projects own behavior onto others
- Excessive talking (talking is a way to avoid feeling empty)
- Clinginess, holding on, not being able to leave, panic at being alone

- Possible addictions or escape mechanisms — substance abuse (cigarettes, alcohol, painkillers), eating disorders (bulimia, overeating), shopping/buying too much stuff, sex addiction, or causing fights or drama to get attention

The Endurer – Triggers, Patterns, Defenses

Common Triggers (For Your Stress)

- Criticism
- Bullying or injustice
- Someone taking advantage of someone on your team or in your family
- Someone violating a boundary
- Someone else's success
- Being the center of attention, called on to speak or perform in front of others
- Being asked to reveal something personal (fear of showing real self)
- Being taken advantage of, being asked to sacrifice something
- Being called "not enough" or "too much"

Energy Stress Patterns (When Triggered)

- Holding in and down into self, compression
- Hiding out/pulling back

Common Emotional Reactions and Defensive Behaviors

- Main emotion when triggered: defeated
- Workaholic behavior (work harder, longer hours)
- Constant complaining
- Passive aggression
- Self-doubt
- Martyrdom and victimization ("why me?" or "poor me")
- Harboring grudges and resentment
- Self-deprecating (easily makes fun of self), uses laughter and humor to mask pain
- Boiling inside but terrified to let it out (feeling like you are "going crazy")
- Lashing out at someone once you have finally "had enough" (cannot contain their bottled-up anger anymore)
- Depression, powerlessness, complete exhaustion
- Possible addictions or escape mechanisms – food, sugar, watching TV (anything that keeps the inertia), alcohol or pain killers to numb the pain of not expressing their real emotions, helping others to avoid helping yourself

The Commander – Triggers, Patterns, Defenses

Common Triggers (For Your Stress)

- Being wrong or being called out as wrong
- Not being in control of a situation, not being able to dominate
- Power being removed
- Criticism of any kind
- Feeling betrayed by someone
- Someone shining a light on a flaw of yours no matter how small

Energy Stress Patterns (When Triggered)

- Energy *out*, dominating and controlling others
- Fight energy (as in "fight or flight")

Common Emotional Reactions and Defensive Behaviors

- Main emotion when triggered: betrayed
- Unforgiving, unable to apologize
- Passive aggressiveness
- Vengeful behavior – lashing out at or punishing someone who has criticized you or brought attention to a flaw of yours
- Bullying, unbending, aggressive or attacking behavior

- Untruthfulness, exaggeration of the truth, gaslighting
- Tendency to blame others for your mistakes (since you cannot be wrong)
- Drives harder than normal, very impatient and manipulative
- Makes impossible demands of team and family members, barking orders at people
- Possible addictions or escape mechanisms – power, control over others, substances that make you feel powerful and in charge, can get addicted to having arguments just to prove you are "right"

The Achiever – Triggers, Patterns, Defenses

Common Triggers (For Your Stress)

- Someone winning against you (beating you)
- Not being perfect or being seen as perfect
- Missing a deadline or your team missing a deadline
- Someone changing plans on you
- Having to be authentic and vulnerable
- Emotions coming to the surface or anyone else showing emotions

Energy Stress Patterns (When Triggered)

- Complete containment – freeze and nothing is getting in or out (like ice)

- Holding in very tightly and evenly throughout the whole body

Common Emotional Reactions and Defensive Behaviors

- Main emotion when triggered: vulnerable
- Driven more than normal
- Obsessively cleaning, organizing or planning
- Being busy all the time, no slowing down, "gotta get things done"
- Working tirelessly for perfection – working hard to get every tiny detail perfect
- Inability to show true self – superficiality, unauthenticity
- Ignoring other's emotions, unable to be truly empathetic when triggered
- Seeing emotional people as being weak
- Possible addictions or escape mechanisms – obsessively exercising, possible addition to plastic surgery (the constant quest for perfection)

Once you write these in your journal or on a piece of paper, you may want to put it in table form. And it will look something like this:

Triggers	Energy Stress Pattern	Reactions/defenses (emotional, behavioral)
Being center of attention	Freeze	Anxiety/worry, nervousness, hurried speech, losing things

Being criticized or bullied	Hold in/Push down	Boiling inside, want to lash out but I just can't
Being taken advantage of, being asked to sacrifice something	Freeze, then Hold in	Boiling inside, workaholism, not setting boundaries or saying no
Someone telling me I did something wrong	Fight, energy *out*	Criticism of the one who criticized me, vengeful behavior
Not being in control of something	Hold in, then push out	Anger, manipulation to ensure I get control

Remember you will put this information up on your wall or somewhere you can see it so you can track over the next week or so. Track when and how often all of these happen so you can be aware of your triggers, patterns and defenses. Every time you notice one, just own it, be OK with it and stay curious about it (no judgement). This one act can diffuse the power the trigger, pattern or reaction has over you.

How was that experience for you? Was it surprising? Did it trigger you? Was it hard to identify your triggers? Did you notice after you outlined some of your triggers that they had less power over you? If so, you may want to write about that in your journal. This awareness of your triggers and reactions is so eye-opening and is the first big step toward losing the sh*t that does not serve you. Truly owning your challenges is so very powerful!

In the next chapter, we will take it a step further at look at "the stories in your head," the true source or programming of your triggers. Let's move on!

LOSE YOUR SH*T

CHAPTER 6: STEP 3 – SHED YOUR STORIES

"Nothing ever goes away until it teaches us what we need to know."

–Pema Chödrön

Now that you have identified and owned your triggers, patterns and reactions, it is time to figure out where they heck they all came from. This is the step where you get the sh*t out of your head.

We are all triggered by different things and our reactions differ. When you are triggered by something, it activates a response or reaction in your head and body and you act on it. The same thing can happen to two different people but they will react two completely different ways. But why? The reason is that your reaction, your pattern is based on your "programming." This programing includes core beliefs that were formed in the different stages of development based on a "trauma" experience or a perceived wound in those stages. Core beliefs were formed at the time of the trauma or wound as defensive measures to protect yourself at that young age and then they became ingrained into you, as if they were true, then and now. It's much like a computer program.

These beliefs may have been true back then, but they are most likely not true at all now. Then throughout your life when things happen to you, those beliefs pop up and stories are created to reinforce those core beliefs. These stories are part of your programming. Identifying these stories, which are really your victim stories (that is, "the sh*t stories in your head"), and getting these stories *out* of your head helps you to look at these stories and recognize that they are not true and how you may be sabotaging yourself.

Sample Stories

Let's look at some examples. For me, I listed stress about money and value as my top challenge. I knew I needed to write out my "money stories": the stories in my head about money. This would be how I felt about money, my experience with money, and perhaps the first experience or relationship with money from my childhood or young adulthood and then another story from a more recent experience about money. This is what I wrote:

"Past story: I grew up with money. My dad was a narcissist, greedy, driven to success, and he loved showing off with money. He was rude, arrogant, and a bully. It was embarrassing to me. I guess I associate being 'successful' and having a lot of money with my father. He would use it as a weapon against us. If we fed his ego, he would reward us with money or material things. If not, we were not (like being punished). So basically, you had to be superficial to *get* rewarded, to be 'of value.' When I was honest and truthful, I was punished. He paid for my brother and sister to go to college, but not me. He said he would, but then he pulled out at the last minute, making up an excuse, making me feel like I had no value at all. This kind of thing happened a lot and was very stressful and depressing to me as a young adult. Because I did not constantly feed my father's ego, I was abandoned by him. We never really had a close relationship because of the money thing. I guess I associate having money and success with being greedy, mean, bullying and rejection."

"More recent story: my former business partner was very greedy and insisted on being CEO of our company (even though I had the company by myself before she joined). She loved wielding power over people, especially me. She was narcissistic and greedy and insisted on being the sales lead and acted like she was the only person bringing in sales and money to the company (which was actually not true). I realized later that I had made more sales than she had. Our company did very well financially, but we had a falling out. I could not deal with her tirades nor feed her ego anymore. I paid her *a lot* of money to leave. Then the industry tanked, and I lost everything."

See the similarities in the stories? When I stopped feeding my dad's narcissistic ego, I lost money (value) and felt worthless. When I stopped feeding my business partner's narcissistic ego and decided to separate from her, I lost my company and all of my money and I felt worthless. There was a core belief that I had to feed someone else's ego and put myself second, to have value, to make money. If I put myself first, I lost. This was definitely a story that I needed to shed.

Last year I had a client who felt like he just had too much pressure on him and that everyone wanted a piece of him and he felt like he was going crazy, like he was going to explode. Randy didn't know what to do. I had him write out the "stories in his head" about responsibilities. Randy's stories are below:

"Past story: I grew up in Harlem and was the second oldest of four and the oldest boy. My single mom worked two jobs, so I had a lot of responsibilities. At age nine, I was responsible for waking up my two younger siblings, feeding them, and taking them to school before I had to go to school. Then I had to go pick them up and walk them home. That was a lot of responsibility for nine years old! If I didn't do everything perfectly, my mom would yell at me. If I reacted at all to the yelling, she would beat me. It was very stressful."

"More recent story: I have two kids by two different exes. I have my three-year-old every other weekend. Because I am a business owner, my hours are more flexible so I pick her up from school every day at 2 p.m., feed her, and spend time with her before dropping her off at her mom's. Every time I drop her off, her mom complains to me that I didn't do this or that right. If I argue, she starts in on the drama and asks me to do all these extra things for her and my daughter, and it is just too much. I love my daughter but I already have so many responsibilities with my business; I don't need this additional drama! Every time I leave there, I feel like I want to bust wide open!" See the similarities? He associated responsibilities with being overwhelmed and being punished.

Your Stories

Okay, now it is your turn. I want you to go back to your challenges and pick one or two that are really bothering you and write your stories about those challenges. Try to write both a past story (preferably childhood or young adulthood) and a more recent story. The more recent, the better. If you are a creative, you can draw or paint your stories or write a little mini-play and act it out. You can even record them.

If you are having a hard time with coming up with what stories to write, you can write some basic stories to get your juices flowing. Below are some common stories that people have in their heads, associated with false core beliefs. I have noted beside some of them which character type they are most common with, if applicable.

Basic story ideas

- Your bio story (how you introduce yourself and tell about your background)
- Your "bad mother" story
- Your "bad father" story

Common Challenge Stories Ideas

- Your money story or relationship with money story
- Your responsibilities story
- Your business failure story
- Your fear (or anxiety) story (Dreamer)
- Your sad story (abandonment, rejection) (Charmer)
- Your "I'm worthless" story (Dreamer)
- Your "I'm not enough" story (Endurer, Charmer)
- Your "I will never have enough" story (Charmer)
- Your "I'm bad" story (Endurer, Charmer)
- Your "I'm ashamed" story (Endurer)
- Your "I'm not perfect" story (Achiever)
- Your jealousy story (Charmer, Commander)
- Your anger or rage story (Endurer, Commander)

- Your resentment story (Endurer, Commander)
- Your envy story (Endurer, Charmer)
- Your betrayal story (Commander)
- Your vulnerability story (Achiever)

Speak Your Stories

Okay, now comes the fun part. I want you to speak these stories aloud to someone. Either your partner, a trusted friend, or colleague. If you are a creative, you can act them out. There is so much power in our stories being witnessed by another person. And if you are *really brave*, you may record a video of it and send it to a trusted person. Who knows? You may even want to publish these stories in a blog. Whatever works for you.

My client Victoria was so afraid to share any of her stories with anyone so she recorded them on video but did not share them with anyone. However she did go back to review the videos of her stories. It was so eye-opening for her as she could really see how she had cast herself as a victim in all of her stories. And she realized that most of the stories were not true anymore. And just like that, she shed those stories. Our stories are very powerful and can control us, our reactions and our behavior without even knowing it. Special note: keep your stories handy as we will use them later in the book.

After you do this step, notice how you feel over the next few days. You should feel lighter just getting those stories out of your head.

Inquire Within

Now let's go "inside" and inquire about your stories and defenses, why they are there, where they came from, and get some answers as to how to shed those stories so that they will no longer hinder you. To help you do that, you are going to create your own inner supervillain or saboteur!

A Little Bit About Heroes and Villains

I believe there are two entities inside you: your supervillain (your shadow or dark side) and your superhero (your higher power or light side). Supervillains are not really bad, just misunderstood. If you think of most supervillains in comic books or movies, they were damaged souls whose defenses or challenges got the better of them.

What if we took your top challenges from what you identified earlier and "assign" them to your own *supervillain* that is "living inside" you? And what if we take all of the positive traits, gifts, and talents of your dominant type(s) and assign those to your own *superhero* living inside you? And what if that could help uncover and repair the damage of those challenges by doing that? What if it could help you become the leader you were meant to be?

Your inner supervillain is a part of you, but it is not the *real* you. It is the one who took the pain, suffered the trauma, created the false beliefs, the defenses, the stories – created your programming. But we do not want to get rid of it – it is a part of you. We just want access to it because it has so much information that can help you. It is not to be feared or ignored; it is to be nurtured.

70

I have done this exercise myself and with many clients, and it is amazing how powerful, expanding, and fun it is! If you are more comfortable using "your light" and "your shadow" instead of superhero or supervillain, feel free. I prefer superhero and supervillain because I am a nerd!

Your Inner Supervillain

Let's start to create your own supervillain; your superhero will come in another chapter. Once you have your supervillain created, you can talk to it – ask it questions, ask it what it wants and why it is here. This is not only fun, but very informative. I know it may sound childish or a little weird, but just go with it! You will be surprised at the answers it will give you!

With that said, let's look back at what you identified earlier, which includes the traits of your dominant type, along with your challenges, patterns, triggers, reactions, and stories and complete the supervillain worksheet below.

Supervillain Work Sheet

Complete the information below in your journal:

- **Name**: give your supervillain a name. You may want to do this after you have filled in more of the sheet.
- **Human/Animal/Sex**: is it human or animal? Is it male or female? Or maybe gender neutral?
- **Physical traits**: what are some of the physical traits you want your supervillain to have? Think of physical traits that you don't like about yourself or

some physical traits from one of your dominant types (chapter 4).

- **Personality traits**: what are some of the negative traits you want to assign to your supervillain? Go back and look to see what you highlighted in chapters 4 and 5. These should be traits that you do not like about yourself or maybe even traits that you really don't like about others. Have fun with it.

- **Your supervillain special powers/your defenses**: what are some of your biggest challenges that you identified earlier? These include your challenges, triggers, reactions, and defenses. Think of ones that are particularly challenging or that you really wish you did not do or have. Those are the good ones! Be as outrageous, nasty and fun as you wish. This is your chance to be really bad!

- **Weapons of choice**: this is for fun and includes any kind of weapon that you think your supervillain would wield. Weapons can be physical things like a sword or maybe even clever ways your supervillain has of sabotaging you – like negative self-talk, procrastination, etc. Again, this is a chance to go all-out! You will continue to add to this as you practice more with your supervillain.

Make it Real

Now that you have documented your supervillain, let's make it real. You need a physical representation to have something to interact with so that you can ask it questions about your stories. To make it real, I suggest one of the following:

- Buy or use an action figure (you can easily get one online or at any toy store or get a personalized one at Etsy)
- Buy or use a stuffed animal
- Draw it or have someone draw it for you
- Try an online generator like heromachine.com to create it and print it out
- Create a sock puppet (decorate it, making eyes and a mouth – have fun with it)

Once you have your supervillain in physical form, you are ready for the inquisition.

The Inquisition

Now comes the fun part – you get to interact with it and ask it questions. You can ask it any question you want, but it is important that you have a witness for "The Inquisition." You may not be able to do that, but it is very beneficial. Keep in mind that you can do this virtually. Try to find a trusted partner, friend, or colleague. Also, make sure you have the list of your patterns, triggers, reactions, defenses, and stories handy, along with your journal or notebook. Keep in mind *you* (as yourself) are asking the questions *to* your supervillain (the physical representation).

Once you have your supervillain (or saboteur) ready, find a quiet place and begin asking it questions. For each question, wait for a reply. Do *not* overthink it; just feel into it and answer the first thing that pops up. Jot down the answers in your notebook. Sample questions are below:

- What do you want? Why?
- What do you need? Why?
- Why does [name a trigger] trigger you?
- Why do you (always) do [name a defense, pattern]? How did this serve you (or me) in the past? How does it serve you (or me) now?
- Tell me about my [name a story] story? Where did it come from? What is the original source of that story? What can I do to change that story?
- How can I let go of that story?
- What will make you feel safe?
- What advice do you have for me?

Example Inquisition

Below is an example inquisition from my client Randy. The responses from his supervillain are in italics.

- What do you want? *I want to be seen, noticed.* Why? *Because you ignore me so much of the time. I try to come out but you push me down.*

- What do you need? *I need to protect you.* Protect me from what? *From those who want to hurt you.* Who wants to hurt me? *Everyone with authority over you. It's not safe. People are not safe.*

- Why does criticism trigger you so much? *Because it means I am not enough or too much. And I feel so much shame when someone criticizes me. I cannot hold shame so I push it down. Or I explode. And then I feel worse.*

- Why is it so hard to admit you are wrong or apologize? *I feel like I cannot be wrong. If I am wrong, I will die or disappear. I won't matter. If I am wrong, mom won't love me anymore.*

- Tell me about my business failure story. Where did it come from? *When I was nineteen and on my own, I got super successful very quickly. Then people took advantage of me. I felt sorry for them so I helped them. But then it backfired and I lost everything. And I lost confidence in my abilities. I learned that I could not trust anyone moving forward. And no one that I have tried to do business with has been trustworthy.*

- What can I do to change or let go of that story? *I don't know.* Who can I trust? *No one.* If I could find someone trustworthy, would you be game to trust them? *Maybe.* What if I find someone and run them by you, are you okay with that? *Yes.*

- What will make you feel safe? *To know that you are okay. That I am doing my job.* And what is that? *Protecting you.* What if I ask you to drop the protection for a while and that I "got this"? *I don't understand. How could this work?* I could check in on you every few days and report back so you know I am okay. Would that suit you? *Yes.*

You can do this exercise any time a new challenge arises. You will be surprised that all of the answers are within you, if you just ask. Remember to take your time with this part of the process. This is fun, but also hard stuff and it is important to go at your own pace. Now that you have gotten a lot of questions answered, let's move on to documenting your limiting beliefs.

Document Your Limiting Beliefs

It is now time to go review everything you have done and look for common threads and document your limiting beliefs. What do I mean by that? Those are the false core beliefs that you formed as a child, the ones that your inner supervillain is operating from. They are your programming and a big part of your "operating system." These beliefs are usually *not* true now, but may still be controlling your life subconsciously and sabotaging you. Your mind will direct you toward things and people to validate these beliefs. For example, if you have a belief that you cannot trust anyone, you will be drawn to people (personal partners, business partners, colleagues, etc.) that are not trustworthy so as to ensure your belief still stands. Documenting these beliefs is the key to "flipping the script" of these beliefs or reprogramming them.

Let's review what you wrote from your inner inquisition with your supervillain. Did you notice some common themes? Did any beliefs come through? Let's review some of the examples from Randy again below. Answers are in italics.

- What do you want? *I want to be seen, noticed.* Why? *Because you ignore me so much of the time. I try to come out but you push me down.*

- What do you need? *I need to protect you.* Protect me from what? *From those who want to hurt you.* Who wants to hurt me? *Everyone with authority over you. It's not safe. People are not safe.*

- Why does criticism trigger you so much? *Because it means I am not enough or too much. And I feel so much shame when someone criticizes me. I cannot hold shame so I push it down. Or I explode. And then I feel worse.*

- Why is it so hard to admit you are wrong or apologize? *I feel like I cannot be wrong. If I am wrong, I will die or disappear. I won't matter. If I am wrong, mom won't love me anymore.*

- Tell me about my business failure story. Where did it come from? *When I was nineteen and on my own, I got super successful very quickly. Then people took advantage of me. I felt sorry for them so I helped them.*

But then it backfired and I lost everything. And I lost confidence in my abilities. I learned that I could not trust anyone moving forward. And no one that I have tried to do business with has been trustworthy.

Looking at some of the themes from Randy's examples, a few limiting beliefs came through, such as:

1. It is not safe to be seen, noticed.
2. Everyone with authority over me wants to hurt me; people are not safe.
3. I am not enough or too much.
4. Criticism equals shame.
5. If I am wrong, I will die or disappear – I won't matter; if I am wrong, mom won't love me anymore.
6. I cannot trust anyone because they will take advantage of me.

Remember that these beliefs are working at the subconscious level so you may not have been fully aware of them, this programming. When I worked with Randy, we went through these one by one and talked about them. I asked the following questions of him:

- Were you aware of these?
- Are they true *now*?
- If they are not true, write down why they are not true. Write down examples from your life now to prove that they aroe not true.

- Then rewrite the beliefs so they reflect what is true now – a reverse statement.

- If some of them are still true, what are some things you can do or put in place to turn them around or let them go?

Below is what Randy did:

1. It is not safe to be seen, noticed. *Not true.* Proof: *I perform standup comedy on a regular basis and am seen and noticed a lot. It is perfectly safe. Reverse statement: it is perfectly safe to be seen.*

2. Everyone with authority over me wants to hurt me. People are not safe. *Still kinda true.* What can you do to improve? *Find an authority figure who I trust or can trust or feel safe around and renew or start a friendship or mentorship.*

3. I am not enough or too much. *Still true.* What can you do to improve? *Have a discussion with my girlfriend or a colleague about this. Ask them if this is true.*

4. Criticism equals shame. *Still true.* What can you do to improve? *Ask someone to roleplay and criticize me. Practice this enough times so that I am okay and do not feel shame about it.*

5. If I am wrong, I will die or disappear. I won't matter. If I am wrong, mom won't love me anymore. *Not true.* Proof: *I am wrong often and I am still alive and my mom still loves me. Reverse statement: it is safe to be wrong. I will not die. And my mom loves me even if I am wrong.*

6. I could not trust anyone because they will take advantage of me. *Not true.* Proof: *I trust my friend Rodney and he has never taken advantage of me.*

Sample Limiting Beliefs

Before doing this activity on your own, let's look at some common limiting beliefs for the different types. Keep this handy as you review your inquisition to document your own limiting beliefs.

Common Belief	Type(s)
I don't matter. If I matter, I may get hurt.	Dreamer
I don't have value. It is not safe to have value.	Dreamer
I feel powerless. I need others to feel powerful.	Charmer
It is safer to be alone.	Dreamer
It is not safe to be seen, hiding protects me.	Dreamer
It is not safe to show my real self. If I show my real self, I may get shamed, abused, or hurt.	Endurer, Dreamer
I cannot trust anyone. If I fully trust someone, they will betray me.	Commander
I cannot be alone. If I am alone, I will be powerless.	Charmer
I will never get my needs met.	Charmer
Nothing is ever enough for me.	Charmer
It is not safe to express my anger.	Endurer
If I truly express my anger, I could kill someone or myself.	Endurer

Common Belief	Type(s)
If I speak up for myself, I will have to surrender and then be defeated.	Endurer
If I speak up, I may get hurt.	Endurer
I cannot be wrong. If I am wrong, I may die.	Commander
If I am wrong, I will not be loved.	Commander
If I am perfect, I am loved.	Achiever
If I am not perfect, I will be rejected.	Achiever
If I am authentic, I will lose love.	Achiever
I have to take care of everyone. If I don't, they won't survive.	Endurer

Your Turn

Review your inquisition and identify some common themes. Then look for some common limiting beliefs and write them down. Review them and ask yourself if they are still true. If so, write down some action items you can do to reverse those beliefs, to let them go, like Randy did. If they are not true, strike through them and rewrite the belief of what is true now (usually the opposite). Post these new beliefs on your wall. Say them aloud every day. Meditate on them. Schedule time when you will do the action items. This is how you reprogram your "operating system."

After my client Randy documented his limiting beliefs, he was able to "flip the script" on some of them and completely let go of some of his victim stories. His whole world changed and he felt such a sense of relief. He rarely got triggered after that, his stress level decreased by half and he was able to let people in and trust them again. It improved his relationship with his ex, his mom and his daughter. It improved his outlook about the future and his business. He even started delegating at work and he had extra time on his hands to spend with his daughter. Shedding your stories can free up so much time and space in your life.

After you are done, journal about this whole experience and see what comes up for you. You may even check in on your supervillain and confirm all of this with him/her/it. Adjust as needed.

How was this experience of documenting and letting go of your stories? Do you feel different? Now that you have documented your limiting beliefs, let's move on to my favorite part of the process – Express Your Stress!

CHAPTER 7: STEP 4 – EXPRESS YOUR STRESS

"Stress is the trash of modern life—we all generate it, but if you don't dispose of it properly, it will pile up and overtake your life."
– Tony Robbins

This chapter is where the rubber meets the road! Now that you are more familiar with what has been behind your stress and your reactions, it is time to change the game! You are going to express your stress and actually "lose your sh*t!" — that is, you are going to purge all the "sh*t" that's in your head and in your body ... *out* of you.

This chapter includes all kinds of activities to do. Some are to be done with a partner (like a roleplay) and some are meant to be done alone. Because some include you getting physical, you may need additional tools or resources to assist you. I have dozens of activities but I cannot include them all here, so I am picking the ones that I think will help you the most. Just go through them and try them out, pick the ones that work best for you. And start practicing them on a regular basis. Some may work, some may not, depending on your character type. The ones that work will change your life drastically and immediately.

Below is a list of the activities in order so you can scroll to find the ones that interest you the most. They are broken out into three categories: 1) **out of head** for getting things out of your head, 2) **out of body** for purging the built-up anxiety and emotions in your body, and 3) **trigger challenges** for helping you address your triggers head on.

1. **Out of Head**
   - The Daily Muck and Shuck
   - Things Left Unsaid
   - The Head Workout
   - Resentment and Fear Inventory
   - The Shame, Guilt and Remorse Inventory

2. **Out of Body**

- o The Purge
- o The Tantrum
- o The Scream
- o The Scream Sing
- o The Mourning
- o The Shame
- o Dance Break
- o Jump for Joy

3. **Trigger Challenges**
   - o Vulnerability Challenge
   - o "Let it Be" Challenge
   - o "Do Nothing" Challenge
   - o Boundaries Excuse Tool
   - o Setting Containers Tool
   - o Delegation Challenge
   - o Criticism Roleplay

Out of Head Activities

The out of head activities are for getting the sh*t out of your head – that includes your fears, limiting beliefs, victim stories, triggers, obsessive thoughts, and negative self-talk.

Activity – The Daily Muck and Shuck (10-15 minutes)

Similar to "Morning Pages" in Julia Cameron's *The Artist's Way*, I do a daily writing practice that I like to call *The Muck and Shuck*. This is something that you can do either first thing in the morning or before you go to bed in the evening. I find if I do it before bed, I can sleep better and I wake up fresh and ready to tackle the day. I take 10-15 minutes and write freehand anything that comes to mind. This is a way of getting all of the "muck" inside your head *out* onto the page where you can "shuck" it (forget it). For me, this includes any negative self-talk, my current worries, things that are making me frustrated or angry, tasks I need to do or forgot to do, or whatever is taking up space in my head that may interfere with my sleep (if done at night) or with being present for the day (if done in the morning). Try it for a few days and experiment with doing it in the evening and then in the morning and see what works best for you. Journal how it helped you (or not).

My client Victoria was very resistant when I suggested that she do this activity every morning. She said she just didn't have the time. I told her to do it for 15 minutes every morning for 3 days in a row as a test and get back to me. She was amazed at the difference it made. Getting all those "shoulds" and worries out of her head first thing in the morning made her day productive with very little stress. She said there is no turning back — now she does it every day.

Activity – Things Left Unsaid (10-15 minutes)

The purpose of this activity is to get out the things that you never said to someone that you really wished you had said. These unsaid things tend to linger in your mind and your body and can really hold you back from embodying your best self. They can hold you back in your life, in your relationships and in your business. Once you write these things down and say them out loud to someone, they lose their power over you. This one exercise can completely change your relationships and give you more confidence.

Instructions:

1. You can do this one of two ways:

    a. *Randomly*: start writing in your journal things you left unsaid, to anyone who pops into mind. For example, "I never told my business partner how much pain he caused me," "I never told Valerie that I loved her," "I never told my sister how much it hurt when she gave away mom's things," or "I never told my boss that I really deserved a raise." Write for as long as you can (usually lasts no more than 15 minutes).

    b. *Focus on one person* and start writing all the things you left unsaid with that person. This works especially well with parents, siblings, past relationships, spouses, current or past business partners, or current or past clients.

2. Write for as long as you can (usually no more than 15 minutes).

3. Extra bonus: after you are done, find a trusted partner and read it aloud. This exercise is very powerful once you read it aloud.

4. Allow yourself time to process any emotions. Journal about it if you need to.

5. This exercise was so effective for my client Randy that he even got enough courage to tell his ex a few

of his unsaid things. And just like that, they had no more power over him and improved their relationship so they can co-parent more effectively.

Activity – The Head Workout (20-30 minutes for 2 people, with a partner)

The Head Workout is specifically for you to get whatever is in your head about a topic out of your head so you can "work it out." For the Workout, you pick a topic, something that has triggered you or is causing you angst, something that you have been trying to "work out" in your head but you are having a problem figuring out a solution alone. You must do this activity with another person, someone you trust (perhaps your partner on this journey). Doing a Workout with someone else (if you both do one) should take about 20-30 minutes, so make sure you have the time and set boundaries around the time. The instructions are simple:

1. There are two roles: the talker and the witness. Decide who is going to go first (who the talker will be).

2. The talker chooses their topic (for example, their business, success, their marriage, money, their anger, etc.).

3. Decide how much time (for example, 5 minutes). The witness sets their timer and asks the talker, "Are you ready to begin your workout on (chosen topic)?"

4. The witness then asks for a statement from the talker by saying, "What do you have on (chosen topic)?"

5. The talker says, "I have (whatever they have on the topic)." Try to be brief and not to go into a long story. Example for a workout on money: "I have that my clients never pay me on time."

6. The witness only responds with "thank you" to each statement (no additional feedback). And then asks for another statement, "What do you have on (topic chosen)?"

7. This is repeated until the timer is up.

8. Witness then asks if they would like more time (no more than 3 extra statements).

9. Once done, the witness asks the talker the following questions: 1) How are you feeling in your body now? Any sensations?, 2) How are you feeling emotionally now? Anything coming up?, 3) Do you notice any new thoughts or beliefs popping up?, and 4) Did any goals or action items about your topic pop up? If so, what are they?

10. Optional: If any goals or action items came up, the talker may want to commit to a day or time to get them (or at least one of them) accomplished. Choose a day to follow up about it.

11. Once done, you switch roles and repeat (if you both are doing a workout).

12. It is important to stay to the timing and the rules and for the witness to not give any feedback to the

talker afterward unless the talker specifically ask for it and you have time. This allows the talker to process the workout in their own way and without judgment.

13. One extra note: after a workout, you may want to journal a bit as lots of ideas, creative thoughts, or goals may emerge after the experience.

This exercise is amazing at helping you work out an issue or problem. I have also found it very helpful to do a regular workout on a specific topic every day for a week or even a month. For example, I did a workout every day for 30 days about money and it completely changed my relationship with money.

Activity – Resentment and Fear Inventory (10 minutes)

Resentment and fear are frequently tied together. This is an activity to document all the resentments and fears going on inside your head. Try to write this on sheets of paper that you can throw away (not in your journal). This is a *great* activity to do every morning or every evening. It can really reduce your stress and anxiety.

Instructions:

1. Complete the following: God (or Universe or Higher Power), I am resentful that _____ because I have fear that I _____.
   Example: *God, I am resentful that my father died when he did because I have fear that I cannot survive handling my business and my family without his support.*

2. Keep going until you run out of steam (5-10 minutes). Write as many fears that are in your head as you can.

3. Once you are done, write the following: God (or Universe or Higher Power), I ask that you remove these resentments and fears. I pray only for knowledge of your will for us and the power to carry that out for me, and (my family, friends, colleagues, and loved ones). (Feel free to name individuals here.)

4. If possible, find a trusted partner or friend and read this aloud to them.

5. Then take the papers you have written on and tear them up and throw them away (or burn them).

6. Journal about this. Or combine this with one of the Out of Body activities (The Purge or The Scream) as this may bring up a lot of buried emotions.

Activity – Shame, Guilt and Remorse Inventory (10 minutes)

Shame, guilt and remorse are frequently tied together. This is an activity to document all the things you are ashamed of, what you feel guilty about and the remorse or regrets you have going on inside your head. Shame is such a complicated and deep emotion. Shame and guilt go hand in hand. Shame almost always comes from the Endurer stage of development (2-3 years gold) when a parent or authority figure made you feel ashamed of something – of being a certain way or doing something. It created a deep wound that you were wrong, you were bad. When that wound is not healed, it gets buried and gains more and more power over the years. And as we age, we may continue to shame ourselves or project our shame onto others and then later we feel tremendous guilt or regret over it. This activity helps release that.

You can write this on sheets of paper that you can throw away or in your journal if you are going to do The Shame activity in conjunction. This is a *great* activity to do in the evening before going to bed. It can really reduce your stress and anxiety.

Instructions:

1. Complete the following on paper:
   "I grew up feeling ashamed of _____
   because my (mother, father, authority figure) did
   (or did not do) _____. As a result I
   feel ashamed of _____. Today I feel
   guilty about _____. I regret that I (did or did
   not do) _____ (list as many things that you
   can think of)."

2. Keep going until you run out of steam (5-10 minutes). Write as many that are in your head as you can.

   Example: I grew up feeling ashamed of my body because my father teased me about being overweight and about maturing early. As a result I still feel ashamed of my body size, no matter what size I am. Today I feel guilty that I blamed myself, made myself and my body "be wrong and bad" and I regret that I lost so many years to low self-esteem as a result.

3. Once you are done, write the following:
   God (or Universe or Higher Power), I ask that you remove these shameful, guilty and remorseful thoughts from me. I pray only for knowledge of your will for me and the power to carry that out for me, and (my family, friends, colleagues, and loved ones).
   (Feel free to name individuals here.)

4. If possible, find a trusted partner or friend and read this aloud to them.

5. Journal about this. Or combine this with one of the Out of Body activities (The Purge, The Mourning or The Shame) as this may bring up a lot of buried emotions.

Out of Body Activities

The activities in the section are designed to get unexpressed emotions *out* of your body. Unexpressed emotions are the cause of so much or our daily stress. The stress that is "always there," lurking around in your body like emotional residue. The most common emotions that can remain in your body are anger/rage/resentment, grief, shame, and anxiety/fear. I will cover each of these.

All unexpressed emotions are still "resident" in your body and can cause extreme stress and serious damage to your health, relationships, your job, your business, your peace of mind, and so on. You will notice that all of these activities are what children *naturally* do to express their emotions. As children, we instinctively know that we need to get these feelings *out* of our body. As we grow up, we are taught that expressing our emotions is "bad" or "wrong" or inappropriate, so we learn to push them down or away. When doing these activities, imagine channeling your inner supervillain or you "inner toddler." Let out everything you were never allowed to do.

In addition, I am covering a joy exercise as well. It is very important to end all activities on a positive note or vibration so you can go on with your day without feeling down or depressed. It is important to move from dark to light every time you do these exercises. Doing these activities on a regular basis will change your life forever. Here we go!

Activity – The Purge (for Rage/Anger/Resentment) (15 or more minutes)

This exercise is for getting out your repressed anger. Most of us are taught that it is not okay to get angry or show anger. This activity is meant for you to embrace and own your inner supervillain, your darkness so that you can purge it. This activity is especially good for Endurer or Commander types.

What is needed for activity (or helpful):

- A tool to use for hitting, like a baseball bat (or a nerf bat), tennis racquet, hockey stick, golf club, or something you can hit your bed or similar kind of soft furniture (something that will not get damaged). You can also use boxing gloves with pads or a punching bag
- A device to play music

- Anger Playlist (2-3 songs to help channel your anger and 1-2 for winding down)
- Comfortable, loose clothing or workout clothes
- Someone there to witness you (if desired)

Instructions:

1. Find a private space and time where you will be alone and can make *a lot* of noise. You can also do this in a group (very helpful to do with others witnessing).

2. Start your anger playlist on your device.

3. Take a couple of deep breaths and feel the music.

4. Embody your rage through your voice and your body– that is, yell, scream, growl, howl, start hitting your bed with your bat (or whatever you choose). Really let it go. No one can hear you. This is safe space. Allow whatever is there to come out. Whatever needs to be said, say it. You may want to picture a person or situation that you are angry at or resentful toward if that helps.

5. Try to go for at least a couple of songs. You won't be able to do it for very long as it is completely exhausting. Grief may come as anger usually leads to grief. Just allow to let whatever comes to come. Be gentle with yourself. You have been holding a lot inside.

6. Wind down with 1-2 songs that will help you feel up and grounded in your body or do the Jump for Joy activity (see later). This is a very important

step so don't skip it. It is important to end on a positive vibration.

7. Try to do a self-care practice after this if you can (massage, nap, or journal).

If you have a lot of built up rage inside of you, this is a good one to do *every day* for a while or at least once a week. Once you get used to it, you will want to do it frequently. It will really keep your system clear of any built up rage.

Activity – The Tantrum (for Rage/Anger/Resentment) (15 or More Minutes)

This exercise is an alternative to the Purge for getting out repressed anger. This is good for anyone who has physical limitations in which it may be hard to do the Purge. Again, this activity is especially good for Endurer or Commander types.

What is needed for activity (or helpful):

- A device to play music
- Anger Playlist (2-3 songs to help channel your anger and 1-2 for winding down)
- Comfortable, loose clothing or workout clothes
- A bed (if possible) or a yoga mat with blankets on the floor

Instructions:

1. Find a private bedroom or space and time where you will be alone and can make *a lot* of noise.
2. Start your Anger playlist on your device.

3. Lay down on your bed or a mat on the floor. Take a couple of deep breaths and feel the music.

4. Embody your rage through your voice and body – that is, yell, scream, growl, howl, and then start throwing a temper tantrum like a child would do. Get your whole body involved, throwing or pumping your arms and legs. Remember you are channeling your inner toddler. Really let it go (but don't hurt yourself!). No one can hear you. This is safe space. Allow whatever is there to come out. Whatever needs to be said or embodied, do it.

5. You won't be able to do it for very long as it is completely exhausting (1-2 songs). Grief may come as anger usually leads to grief. Just allow to let whatever comes to come.

6. Slowly get up from the bed and wind down with 1-2 songs that will help you feel good and present in your body or do the Jump for Joy activity (see later in the chapter). This is a very important step so don't skip it.

7. Try to do a self-care practice after this if you can (massage, nap, or journal).

Activity – The Scream (for Fear or Anxiety) (10 or More Minutes)

This tool is for getting out repressed fear and anxiety. This is especially good for Dreamer and Achiever types. This activity is meant to be done alone (no witnesses).

Instructions:

1. Find a private space and time where you will be alone and can make a lot of noise. This can be done in your home – perhaps in a bedroom, bathroom, closet, or other private, quiet place, like in your car. It's even better if you can find a place outside in nature, but ensure that you will not be heard as people may call the police on you!

2. Then try to scream as loud as you can. This can be a scream, howl, growl, moan, whatever. Think of a primal scream. Try to really embody the scream. Try originating the sound from deep inside your body (belly or lower abdomen). That helps get in touch with that fear and anxiety that resides deep in your body. Think of the scream a newborn baby makes if that helps you. If it hurts your vocal cords or you cannot make that much noise, use a small pillow to muffle the scream. The important thing is to get it out of your body, not how much noise you make.

3. Try stomping your feet or moving your whole body too if you can. Like a child would when trying to get your attention.

4. Between screams, try saying affirmations like, "I am here. I belong here. I matter. I am valued, I am worthy. It is safe to connect with others. The world is a safe place. It feels really good to be seen, to be noticed." Use whatever resonates with you.

5. Other emotions may come to the surface doing this, such as anger or grief. Just allow whatever

comes to come. You can combine this activity with the Purge or the Mourning.

6. Once you are done, put on some soothing music to get present in your body, and move, dance, or do the Jump for Joy activity (see later). This is a very important step so don't skip it.

7. Try to do a self-care practice after this if you can (bath, massage, nap, or journal).

Activity –The Scream Sing (for Fear or Anxiety) (10 or More Minutes)

This tool is for getting out repressed fear and anxiety. This is an alternative for The Scream and is good for all types, most especially Dreamers and Achievers. It can be done alone or with others. What do I mean by "scream sing"? Scream singing is actually singing a song in a very powerful way, like you are screaming it. For example, my favorite Scream Sing song is *Zombie* by the Cranberries. It is a powerful song about the cost of war and it really brings out all of my emotions when I sing it. "Scream singing" is such a powerful release and you can have fun doing it as well. You can even do a group "Scream Karaoke" if that suits you.

What is needed for activity (or helpful):

- A device to play music
- Scream Playlist (2-3 powerful songs you love and can actually "scream sing" to)
- Comfortable, loose clothing or workout clothes

Instructions:

1. Find a private space where can make a *lot* of noise. This can be done in your home – perhaps in a bedroom, bathroom, closet, or other private, quiet place, like in your car.

2. Start your Scream playlist on your device.

3. Take a couple of deep breaths and feel the music.

4. Then start singing to the song as loud as you can. Really belt it out. Scream it if you can. Try originating the sound from deep inside your body (belly or lower abdomen). That helps get in touch with that fear and anxiety that resides deep in your body. Do not care how you sound – no one can hear you. The important thing is to get that residual stress out of your body, not how much noise you make or how you sound.

5. Try stomping your feet or moving your whole body too if you can. Like a Rockstar would. Or like a child would when trying to get your attention.

6. Powerful emotions may come to the surface doing this, such as anger or grief. Just allow whatever comes to come. Try to continue singing the song with whatever emotion comes up. You can combine this activity with the Purge or the Mourning if it feels right.

7. Once you are done, put on some soothing music to get present in your body, and move, dance, or do the Jump for Joy activity (see later). This is a very important step so don't skip it.

8. Try to do a self-care practice after this if you can (bath, massage, nap, or journal).

Activity – The Mourning (for Grief, Loss) (15 or More Minutes)

This tool is for getting out *repressed grief*. This is especially good for Dreamer, Charmer, or Achiever types. This activity is about mourning a loss, no matter how big or how small. We have all suffered losses but not all of us know how to grieve the losses. This activity is meant to be done alone, but if you want witnesses, please do what is comfortable for you. This is also an important one for men to do. All children cry, no matter if they are boys or girls. But boys are told crying is a weakness. Crying is simply a way to release grief and tension out of your body. It is a natural thing to do, a cleanse. And it can greatly reduce worry and anxiety.

What is needed for activity (or helpful):

- A device to play music
- Grief Playlist (2-3 songs to help encourage your sadness or grief to emerge and 1-2 for winding down)
- Tissues

Instructions:

1. Find a private space and time where you will be alone and can make some noise. This can be done in your home or in your car.
2. You can stand, sit, or even lay down.

3. Start your Grief Playlist. Or you put on a sad movie.

4. Embody your grief through your voice and body—
    that is, cry, wail, howl, and move your body slowly
    back and forth if that feels right. If you need to
    scream, then scream. But be gentle and caring with
    yourself. This is safe space. Allow whatever is there
    to come out. Whatever needs to be said or
    embodied, do it.

5. Do this for as long as you can (no more than 2-3
    songs). Grief is almost as tiring as anger so be
    gentle with yourself. Allow yourself to release the
    grief, to mourn your losses. Remember that you
    have been physically carrying this grief in your
    body for a while and it needs to come out.

6. Slowly wind down with 1-2 songs that will help
    you feel good and present in your body or do the
    Jump for Joy activity (see later in chapter). This is a
    very important step so don't skip it. It is important
    to end on a positive vibration.

7. Try to do a self-care practice after this if you can
    (massage, nap, or journal).

Activity – The Shame (for Shame, Guilt, Remorse) (20 or More Minutes)

This tool is for getting out *repressed shame, guilt or remorse.*
This is especially good for Endurer types. This activity is
about getting in touch with and letting go of buried shame,
guilt and remorse. You may want to do the Shame, Guilt
and Remorse Inventory first before you do this activity.

This activity is meant to be done alone, but if you want witnesses, please do what is comfortable for you. This is also an important one for men to do. This activity can also greatly reduce worry and anxiety.

What is needed for activity (or helpful):

- Your journal and a pen
- A device to play music
- Shame Playlist (2-3 songs to help encourage your shame or regret to emerge and 1-2 for winding down). I use a combination of songs from both my anger and grief playlists, but do what is right for you.
- A picture of you between the ages of 2-8 if you have one.
- Tissues

Instructions:

1. Find a private space and time where you will be alone and can make some noise. This can be done in your home or in your car.

2. If you have done the Shame, Guilt and Remorse Inventory, take that out and review it. If you have not, then take out your journal and start writing "I am ashamed of _____. I feel guilty about _____. I have remorse or regrets about _____." Name as many things as you can.

3. Get out the photo of yourself and look at that little girl or boy. Think about him or her.

4. Start your Shame Playlist. Embody your shame or guilt through your voice and body– that is, scream, rant, rave, cry, wail, howl, and move your body however feels right. Think about that little girl or boy and try to feel what they felt. But remember to be gentle and caring with yourself. This is safe space. Allow whatever is there to come out. Whatever needs to be said or embodied, do it.

5. Do this for as long as you can (no more than 2-3 songs). Allow yourself to release the shame, guilt, remorse, anger, grief, loss, whatever comes up. Remember that you have been physically carrying this shame and guilt in your body for a while and it needs to come out.

6. Slowly wind down with 1-2 songs that will help you feel good and present in your body or do the Jump for Joy activity (see later in chapter). This is a very important step so don't skip it. It is important to end on a positive vibration.

7. Try to do a self-care practice after this if you can (massage, nap, or journal).

Activity –Dance Break (5-10 Minutes)

This exercise is just a simple embodiment exercise – dancing, moving your body. This is especially good for anyone who has a sedentary job. You can easily do this between meetings or calls. It is especially helpful to do before an important meeting or call as it gets you fully present in your body and you will most likely be able to make more effective decisions. You can even do this activity as a group with your team, in person or on a call. I started doing this with my team and it is so much fun! Everyone looks forward to the dance break!

What is needed for activity:

- A device to play music
- Dance Playlist (1-2 upbeat songs that you can do to, that really make you feel alive and happy)

Instructions:

1. Start your dance playlist.
2. Feel the music and move your body - slow or fast, whatever works.
3. You can do this standing up or sitting in a chair.
4. Do this for a song or two.

If you do this activity every day, you will feel a tremendous difference in your stress level and productivity.

Activity – Jump for Joy (for Positive Energy) (15 or More Minutes)

This exercise is for channeling joy and positive energy. This is especially good to do after any of the other activities in this section and is good for all types. It helps get you present in your body and turn any negative emotion to positive so that you can "go on with your day" feeling good. This exercise can be done at any time – like before an important meeting, presentation, or performance as it really helps reduce stress and improve your state of mind. You can do this activity alone or with others. Once you introduce this activity to your friends or colleagues, they will want to do it every day!

What is needed for activity (or helpful):

- A device to play music
- Joy Playlist (1-2 upbeat songs that really make you feel alive and happy)
- Comfortable clothing and fitness shoes (or barefoot is even better)
- Soft flooring or a yoga mat. Or if you have access to a trampoline or mini-trampoline, this would be *ideal.*

Instructions:

1. Find a private space and time where you will be alone and can make some noise. This can be done in your home or at work (in a private office, closet, or bathroom) or outside in nature on grass. The best scenario is at home or outside on a mini-trampoline.
2. Start your Joy Playlist on a music device.
3. Take a couple of deep breaths and feel the music.
4. Then raise your hands up in the air (above head), start jumping up and down (like a kid) and say, "Yes! Yes! Yes!" over and over. You are approving and saying yes to all things in your life (good and bad). You can even say things like, "Yes to my life. Yes to my business. Yes to money flowing to me. Yes to my health. Yes to my relationship. Yes to my breakup. Yes to my successes. Yes to my failures."

Whatever comes to mind. Think like a kid who is so excited and is jumping for joy!

5. Try speaking any other joyous sentiments that come to mind, such as, "I love me. I love my life. I love my partner. I love my business. I love my clients. All of life comes to me with joy, ease, and glory."

6. Do this for as long as you can (no more than 2 songs). You will be amazed at how you feel during and after this activity. You will get a rush of endorphins.

7. You can choose to wind down from this, but I find that I feel so good that I don't want to!

If you do this activity every day, you will feel a tremendous difference in your stress level, productivity and overall happiness. It is better than any drug you could take!

Trigger Challenges and Tools

The activities in this section are designed to activate some of your triggers to see if they trigger you and what your reaction is. If you are still triggered, then that means you need to practice these challenges so that the trigger becomes less and less powerful over time. Scroll through these and see which ones you want to work on.

Vulnerability Challenge

Vulnerability or being vulnerable is especially difficult for Endurers, Commanders, and Achievers.

For one week, try being vulnerable once a day – with someone safe like your partner or a close family member. Then try doing it with a trusted friend or colleague. An example would be to share something that you are afraid of or that causes you anxiety, like, "I get anxious when things are not perfect. I feel like I have to correct other people's work when it is not perfect. I know I shouldn't, but I can't help it" or "I don't think my employees like me and that really bothers me" or "I am sometimes afraid that I am going to get fired because I don't really like my job anymore and I think it shows." Remember, "being vulnerable" is really just being authentic, just showing the *real* you.

After doing this activity, journal what you notice and how you feel. Did it create anxiety? Did anything change? Did people treat you differently? Journal what happened and what you notice.

"Let It Be" Challenge

This activity is especially good for both Endurers and Achievers. Endurers have a tendency to want to rescue others and Achievers have a hard time with any kind of "a mess" – both physical and other (like projects at work).

For one week, try *not* to clean up anyone else's mess – to just "let it be." For example, if your teenage kids made a mess in the house, ask them to clean it up. If they don't, leave it. Another example would be if you are working on a project at work with someone and they have made a "mess of it." Try *not* to fix it and just let it be and see what happens. Did it create anxiety? Did anything change as a result? Did they fix their own mess because you didn't do it for them? Did people treat you differently? Journal what happened and what you notice.

"Do Nothing" Challenge (15-30 minutes)

Achievers have a hard time sitting still and doing nothing, just *being*. Schedule time in your calendar for time to literally "Do Nothing." That is, to just chill, sit on the couch, meditate, whatever. Do not read or watch TV. Do not get on your phone or social media. Do not do any work or any chores. Do not take a nap. This has to be awake time of "doing nothing" and being present with yourself. This is very *hard* for Achievers.

Start with once a day (if you can) for 15-30 minutes and see how you feel. Journal what you notice. Did it create anxiety? Do you feel guilty about doing nothing? Did anything change?

Boundaries Excuse Tool (10-15 minutes)

Setting boundaries is especially hard for the Endurer type. Endurers have a hard time setting boundaries with others because they do not want to disappoint anyone. They end up saying "yes" to all kinds of things that they do not need or want to do, usually because they have a hard time saying no, they really enjoy helping people and they cannot think quick on their feet with an "excuse." That is why I created the Boundaries Excuse List.

You can use this list as a kind of "cheat sheet" when someone asks you to do something that you do want to do, do not have time or energy to do, or is not in your best interest to do. Below is a sample list from my client Jan:

- No, I am sorry I cannot. (No need to say anything more. This one is really hard for a lot of people!)

- I am working on setting boundaries, and this is not something that would be in my best interest to do right now. But I appreciate you asking me.

- This does not fit with my goals for the year. I really appreciate you asking. Why don't you ask _____ instead?

- I am not the best fit for this task as my plate is already full. Why don't you ask _____ to help you out?

- I am not the best qualified person for this. I would ask _____ to help you out.

- I would love to take you on as a client, but I am only taking on clients that (fit in with my strategy and vision for the future). I recommend that you contact _____ instead.

- I would love to, but I am only going to events that really jazz me and this does not really do that. Thank you for asking and have fun!

- That sounds like fun, but I had planned to stay home tonight for some down time (or to paint), and I am going to stick to that plan. I hope you enjoy yourself.

- (For a date that you did not want to go on) I like you, but I don't see us being a match and I do not want to waste your time or my time. But thank you for asking. I wish you the best.

Now create your own list and have it handy so you can use it. Keep in mind the excuse has to be true to use it! This is a really fun list to create. Practice these for 2 weeks and see if it gets easier and easier to set boundaries. Journal about your experience. By the way, setting up this list and using it can also help you lost weight. Sounds crazy but it works!

Setting Containers Tool

This tool is good for any type, but especially for Endurers. A container is a set of expectations, rules, or boundaries that you set up for things like a relationship, an event, a meeting, or even a conversation. Setting a container is very important in certain situations, especially as a business owner.

For example, you may meet up with someone (client, colleague, vendor, employee, date) for a very specific reason and then the meeting goes in a completely different direction than you had anticipated. The other person may say something that offends you or makes an odd suggestion, making it hard to get back on track and make it very awkward for you both.

Setting a container for something like this can be very powerful. Here is what a container for that type of scenario might look like: "John, I would like to set up a container for this meeting. We are here to talk about work, and I would like to stick to work topics. I have 30 minutes. Does that work for you?" You can set the container at the beginning of the meeting/event or even when it starts to go off track.

Explore setting containers for certain conversations to start with and see how it works. You will start to recognize when setting a container will help you. I find it works really well for conversations with people who tend to talk too much and take up too much of your valuable time. Here is a simple example: "Mom, I have 10 minutes to talk, what is going on?" Feel free to set a timer and then after the 10 minutes, you can say something like, "It's been 10 minutes, I have to go now." Be very clear and *stick* to the container.

Practice doing this for conversations for one week. Then move onto meetings, events, and even relationships. Journal your experience with it. This is a very powerful tool.

Delegation Challenge

Delegating tasks is especially difficult for Endurers and Dreamers, but it is an essential skill as a business owner and a leader.

For one week, try delegating something once a day to someone on your team – it has to be something you don't normally delegate like meeting with a vendor or leading a meeting. After a week, journal what you noticed and how you felt. Did it create anxiety? Did anything change? Did people treat you differently? If things went well, try delegating more and more tasks each week and see how it goes. Once you are comfortable delegating, you will see how much easier your life will get. And keep in mind that delegating builds leadership skills in others so it helps both parties out.

Criticism Challenge Roleplay (10-15 minutes, with a Partner)

Handling criticism is especially difficult for Endurers, Charmers, and Commanders, but it is an essential skill as a leader and business owner.

1. Make a list of things that *really* bother you about yourself and things that you are sensitive about. These can be things like your weight, looks, performance, products or services, how much money you make, the quality of your work, your success (or lack of it), and so on.

2. Then come up with critical statements or questions that if someone said to you, they would really trigger you. Write those statements or questions down.

3. Then find a trusted partner and have them roleplay with you and say those criticisms to you.

4. For each one, initially try to come back with the first natural response, no matter what it is. Notice how you felt, inside your body. Tell your partner how you felt.

5. Then have them say it again, but this time try to respond by either completely owning the criticism (as if it were actually true). Again notice how you felt, inside your body. Discuss with your partner.

6. Then have them do it a third time and respond by asking a question of them using "you" instead of "I" in your question. Put the focus on the other person, instead of yourself. And notice how you feel. You may feel much less triggered when you have the right responses. Let's look at few examples below:

- **Question**: have you gained weight?
- *Sample answer*: it sounds like you are sensitive about your weight. Is that correct?
- **Question**: how much money do you make?
- *Sample answer*: why is it important for you to know that? What made you ask that question?
- **Statement**: I was not impressed with your service.
- *Sample answer*: it sounds like our service did not meet your needs. What would meet your needs?
- **Question**: you were so wrong about _____. What do you have to say about that?
- *Sample answer*: you are right and I was wrong. Can you tell me what you would have done differently?

Once you practice this enough, you will notice that the criticisms do not bother you as much and that you can handle just about anything anyone throws at you.

My client Randy was so sensitive to criticism. It was a big trigger for him and he would react in an attacking manner. After doing this roleplay with him several times, he got to the point where he welcomed criticism and was ready to respond to anyone in a balanced manner. It has not bothered him since.

Another tip about responding to written criticism is to do a dance break before you respond to it. A dance break will help you get grounded and you can more easily respond to it. And remember, you do not have to respond to all criticism. Once you are no longer triggered, it really does not matter if you respond or not. You can just let it go.

We have reached this end of this chapter. It was a lot, wasn't it? How are you feeling? Was it challenging, rewarding, frustrating, fun, or too much? Did you learn more about yourself? Do you feel different? Try to make notes in your journal about which activities or tools worked best for you. This is a chapter that you can go back through again and again.

Now that you have practiced effectively expressing your stress, you should feel so much lighter and more powerful and resilient. Moving forward is going to be so much easier now. Let's move on to restoring your brilliance and igniting your superpowers!

CHAPTER 8: STEP 5 – IGNITE YOUR SUPERPOWERS

"We all have those things that even in the midst of stress and disarray, they energize us and give us renewed strength and purpose. These are our passions."
– Adam Braun

In this chapter, you will look back at your dominant type and identify your greatest gifts and talents and decide which ones you want to ignite and fully own to truly be the leader you were meant to be, the leader the world needs you to be. These are your superpowers! To facilitate this, you are going to create your inner superhero like you did earlier with your inner supervillain.

Passion Check-In

Now that you have done all of this work on defeating your stress, new desires and passions may start to arise and it is important to document those before moving forward. No matter what your career is or what your business is, it is important to live a life of passion. If your business is not your passion or does not include a passion of yours, you will not be truly successful and it will always cause you some kind of stress (not living your passion in some way). Your superpowers must include passion, otherwise they would just be skills.

With that in mind, let's do a quick passion check-in. You may already "know" all of this stuff about yourself, but just go with me on this. Sit back, relax, close your eyes, and regulate your breathing for about one minute. Quiet your mind. Now ask yourself, "What do I really want?", "What are my greatest desires?", "What do I love to do?", and "What do I want to be known for?" Whatever comes up, write it down. Make a list for each question. They could be things like writing a book, scuba diving, traveling around the world, cooking, teaching others, making the world a better place, painting, singing, and so on. Then for each one of them, do a three-body check-in (from the end of chapter 3) where you check-in with your physical body for any sensations, your emotional body for any emotions coming up, and your mind for any thoughts or beliefs that are triggered or come up. Write down everything you notice. You should have 3-5 big passions come up. Now keep all those handy. Let's move on to creating your superhero.

Your Inner Superhero

It is now time to create your own inner superhero focusing on your strengths, gifts, and talents (your superpowers), but also adding some strategies to battle your inner supervillain. So, let's look at the gifts and talents for each type and identify your top 10 you want to own – that is, the talents that you currently use and are most proud of, as well as the ones you are passionate about and are inside you but maybe you have not had a chance to use lately or have not cultivated them yet.

Then let's identify what "weapons of choice" you will use to fend off your supervillain. That is, what practices you will arm yourself with to strengthen your superhero.

Below are some of the main talents and gifts of each type along with suggested activities or self-care practices that would help to support your true self. Look through these to get some ideas of talents you want to own, and come up with your own list – perhaps more specific to your experience, your industry, your business, your passion, etc.

The Dreamer – Talents in a Nutshell

- **True essence**: creativity
- **Natural talents**: brilliance, innovation, visionary, independent, artistic, intuitive, innovative problem-solver, animal lover, nature lover, performer (music, singing, dancing), idea person, inventor
- **Suggested self-care practices**: do a resentment and fear inventory daily or weekly; grounding meditation; deep breathing; move your body; dance; connect with another human being (on phone or in person); hug someone (ask for hugs!); make a plan of action – walk through the fear; sensorial things – a warm bath, massage, touch, aromatherapy; spend time with animals; spend time in nature; use a weighted blanket; do anything that makes you feel like you are part of this earth and belong here; get a "support buddy" who you can call or be in person with; set safe containers and boundaries for your interactions with others; make your physical environment safe and comfortable (design, colors, lighting furniture, clutter); schedule time to release emotions out of the body in a safe manner and safe space; practice the Head Workout regularly; do the Scream or Scream Sing weekly; do the Jump for Joy daily

The Charmer – Talents in a Nutshell

- **True essence**: love
- **Natural talents**: charm, persuasiveness, teaching, speaking, writing, performing, acting, selling, marketing, collaborating with others/team player, superb spokesperson, master at public relations, publishing, and social media
- **Suggested self-care practices**: ask yourself, "what do I need?"; grounding; deep breathing; take a hot bath; sunbathe; go for a walk; feed the senses – music, art, being in nature; integrate with words; set boundaries; get a massage or other forms of bodywork; go for a swim (breast stroke); take a dance class; do yoga; schedule time to release emotions out of the body in a safe manner and safe space; practice the Head Workout regularly; do The Mourning weekly; do the Jump for Joy daily

The Endurer – Talents in a Nutshell

- **True essence**: compassion
- **Natural talents**: kind, empathetic, giving, nurturing, intuitive, sensitive, thoughtful, helping others, productive, dedicated, loyal, adaptable, a great team leader, compassionate leader, defender of the underdog, teacher, coach, counselor, healer
- **Suggested self-care practices**: do a resentment and fear inventory every day; do a shame, guilt, and remorse inventory once a month; experiment with telling people no; practice setting boundaries;

disidentify with the inner critic – ask "Who is saying that?" in your head – your father, mother, sister, brother; practice forgiveness with family members; do anger therapy (practice the Purge frequently); practice setting boundaries and containers; schedule time to release emotions out of the body in a safe manner and space; practice the Head Workout regularly; do The Purge weekly; do The Shame monthly; practice the Criticism Challenge roleplay regularly; do the Jump for Joy daily

The Commander – Talents in a Nutshell

- **True essence**: leadership
- **Natural talents**: fearless leader, devoted leader, visionary, loyal, brave, charisma, risk-taker, entrepreneurial, confident, adventurous, passionate, spontaneous, great speaker, inspiring, master manifester, driven
- **Suggested self-care practices**: practice letting someone else lead or take the reins from you (on a project or at home); practice apologizing to someone (even if you do not believe you need to); practice admitting you are wrong to someone (even if you do not believe you are right); do a shame, guilt, and remorse inventory once a month; practice the Purge or Tantrum weekly; practice the Shame monthly; grieve over lost childhood; write a letter to your parents (that you do not send); make a plan; work out at the gym; do a dance break; fast-

walk in nature; schedule time to release emotions out of the body in a safe manner and space; do the Scream or Scream Sing regularly; practice the Head Workout regularly; practice the Criticism Challenge roleplay, the Vulnerability Challenge, and the Delegation Challenge weekly; Practice either the "Do Nothing" Challenge or "Let it Be" Challenge regularly; do the Jump for Joy daily

The Achiever – Talents in a Nutshell

- **True essence**: integrity
- **Natural talents**: fairness, balance, quality, beauty, organization, healthy boundaries, high morals and values, organized, planning/project management, detail-oriented, athletic, disciplined, competitive, driven, perfectionist
- **Suggested self-care practices**: do the three-body check-in every day; get massages; share your feelings with your partner, friends, family; ask others to reflect your emotions back to you; let someone else win and see how that feels; practice the "Let it Be" challenge and the "Do Nothing" challenge regularly; practice the Vulnerability Challenge weekly; do the Jump for Joy daily

Superhero Work Sheet

Now let's complete the worksheet below in your journal.

- **Name**: give your superhero a name. You may want to do this after you have filled in more of the sheet.

123

- **Human/Animal/Sex**: is it human or animal? Is it male, female, gender neutral?

- **Physical Traits**: what are some of the physical traits you want your supervillain to have? Think of physical traits that you like about yourself or some physical traits you like in other people or traits you wish you had.

- **Personality Traits**: what are some of the positive traits you want to assign to your superhero? Go back to chapter 4 and look to see what you highlighted. These should be traits that you like or even love about yourself or maybe even traits that you wish you had. Add some spice and some fun.

- **Your superhero special powers/your gifts**: what are some of your greatest talents or skills? Look at your dominant type above or go outside the box. Think of ones that you really want to use or cultivate. What are your passions? What do you really want to be known for? You can even add some fun special powers like superheroes have (invisibility, superhuman strength, ability to fly, etc.). Be as outrageous as you wish. This is your chance to be really fun and cool!

- **"Weapons of choice"/strategies for tackling your supervillain defenses**: this is for fun and can include any kind of weapon that you think your superhero would wield. Weapons can be physical things (like swords, ray guns, fireballs, dragons, whatever) or maybe clever ways your superhero has of defeating your supervillain or ways to support you and your success. Look at the specific self-care practices for your dominant type above or any activities that helped with tackling your triggers and defenses in previous chapters. Again, this is a chance to go all-out! You will continue to add to this as you practice more .

Making it Real

As with your supervillain, you will want to create a physical copy of your superhero. This could be either an action figure, a stuffed animal, a drawing, a printout of an online-generated one, or a decorated sock puppet. It is important to have something physical to interact with.

Once you have it physically, you now have both your supervillain and superhero! Guess what? They can now have a conversation!

We Need to Talk

Now let's do an activity with both your supervillain and superhero. It is important to do this with another person (witness) either in person or virtually as it helps bring the answers forward easier. Have your list of passions handy for this activity.

Activity – The Super Talk (20-30 minutes, with a partner, in person or through video chat)

Find a trusted partner and have the physical representations of your superhero and supervillain ready to have a conversation. Once ready, each of "them" will take turns and act out the following:

1. Your superhero will ask your supervillain any of the following questions. The supervillain will respond with whatever immediately comes up (feel free to change the questions).

   o What do you truly want? Why? (write it down)

   o How does that help (your name)?

   o How can I help you satisfy that want?

   o Are you comfortable with (your name)'s desire of (name one big passion or desire you identified earlier)?

   o If not, why does that make you uncomfortable?

- How can you support (your name) in making those desires come true?
- What gifts or talents of yours do you want to use? Which ones will serve you the most?
- How will these gifts and talents serve (your name) in their business?
- What will make you feel empowered? Why?
- How can I support you? How can (your name) support you?
- What additional advice do you have for me or for (your name)?

2. Then flip it and have the supervillain ask the superhero the same questions.

3. Discuss the experience with your partner.

4. If you are doing this with a partner who wants to participate, then take turns and repeat (where the witness becomes the participant and vice versa).

Now you can have a conversation between the two of them whenever you want and know that they are both there to support you in living the life you came to live, in being the leader you were meant to be! This is an incredible exercise to do on a regular basis whenever you are stuck in any situation, when something is really bothering you or stressing you and you do not see a way forward – whether in your business or your personal life. Be sure to make plenty of notes during this exercise. Some information may not make sense at first but may later. It is always great to have these notes to refer to later.

You will be so surprised how much information you can get from this one exercise – my clients have gained so many "aha" moments doing this exercise.

Adjust both your supervillain and superhero worksheets as necessary to always be up-to-date with where you are. Remember that tackling your triggers and defenses and defeating your stress is a process and takes time and practice. But having all of these tools and practices to choose from really helps give you a jumpstart. Many of us may still need to go see practitioners such as business coaches, psychotherapists, mind-body practitioners, and body workers to continue our journey to success, emotional freedom, wholeness, and aliveness.

How was this exercise for you? Was it fun, interesting? Do you feel different? Try to journal every day for a week after this to see what has changed for you. Do you feel more like yourself? Are you calmer and more confident than before?

Update Your Stories

Now let's take a look back at the stories that you wrote in chapter 6, evaluate where you are now with those stories, and update them with new insights or rewrite them to create entire new stories with you, not as the victim, but as the hero. Rewriting these stories as hero stories instead of victim stories can rewire your brain and literally flip the script on your old programming and beliefs.

Randy's Stories

Let's take a look back at Randy's stories and see what happened when he rewrote his stories after doing the work.

Previous past story: "I grew up in Harlem and was the second oldest of four and the oldest boy. My single mom worked two jobs so I had a lot of responsibilities. At age nine, I was responsible for waking up my two younger siblings, feeding them, and taking them to school before I had to go to school. Then I had to go pick them up and walk them home. That was a lot of responsibility for nine years old! If I didn't do everything perfectly, my mom would yell at me. If I reacted at all to the yelling, she would beat me. It was very stressful."

Updated past story: "I grew up in Harlem and was the second oldest of four and the oldest boy. My single mom worked two jobs, and because I was so industrious, I took on a lot of responsibilities. At age nine, I was responsible for waking up my two younger siblings, feeding them, and taking them to school before I had to go to school. Then I had to go pick them up and walk them home. We had so much fun, walking home. We would walk by my friend Kevin's house where he and his homies were hanging out on the stoop. I was always clowning around and I would try out some new jokes. I was only nine, but I was funny! That was always the highlight of my day. Sometimes I would get in trouble with my mom for being late, but I could always make her laugh and then she would stop yelling. The laughter always beat the stress away!"

Previous more recent story: "I have two kids by two different exes. I have my three-year-old every other weekend. Because I am a business owner my hours are more flexible, I pick her up from school every day at 2 p.m., feed her, spend time with her before dropping her off at her mom's. Every time I drop her off, her mom complains to me that I didn't do this or that right. If I argue, she starts in on the drama and asks me to do all these extra things for her and my daughter, and it is just too much. I love my daughter but I already have so many responsibilities with my business, I don't need this additional drama! Every time I leave there, I feel like I want to bust wide open!"

Updated more recent story: "I have two kids by two different exes. I have my three-year-old every other weekend. Because I am a business owner, my hours are more flexible and I get to pick her up from school every day at 2 p.m. and spend time with her before dropping her off at her mom's. She and I have so much fun after I pick her up. We go to Dave and Busters, we play games, we go to the movies, and we make funny videos. She is always clowning around and we make a pretty good comedy team. She brings me so much joy and laughter and I am so lucky to be her father. When we are together, I have her make something special for her mom and now when I drop her off, her mom is so delighted to get a special gift that she has no complaints. She has stopped asking me to do all of these extra things. The stress and drama in my life has been greatly reduced and I have more time and energy to devote to my business, which is now booming! I love my life."

Once Randy rewrote his stories, he saw how much his life had changed and what stories he now wanted to own. He had much less stress, realized he had let go of the resentment for his ex, and had more time to spend with his daughter. He was sleeping better, has lost weight and his business was now booming.

Your Updated Stories

Now it is time to look back at your stories that you created in chapter 6 and see how they have changed. Ask yourself the following questions:

1. Look at the past story and notice how you see things differently.

2. Look to see where you can change things so that you are no longer a victim in the story, but actually actively making choices. Look at it from how it now benefited you, instead of hindered you. Maybe that story is one of the reasons you have some amazing skill or developed one of your passions. Be grateful to that story for bringing that to life.

3. Now rewrite that story with that in mind.

4. Read it aloud to someone or publish it. Get it out there. It is your new perspective.

5. Now look at your more recent story. How has that changed? With all the work you have done, I bet that story now has a positive spin on it. You are the hero of this story, not the victim.

6. Rewrite that story to include that positive spin. And again, read it aloud to someone – or record it and watch it.

Create Your New Super Stories

If you really want to get creative, write new stories that star you as the hero, maybe even your superhero. Perhaps create your superhero's origin story or new success stories. Again, if you are a creative, feel free to draw, paint, or act out these stories. Have fun with this! Some ideas for new stories include:

- Your creative genius story
- Your amazing mother/father story
- Your generosity story
- Your value story
- Your passion story
- Your rescue story (where you rescue someone or something)
- Your intuition story
- Your bravery story
- Your leadership story
- Your vulnerability story
- Your integrity story
- Your "I'm amazing" story
- Your new introduction story
- Your business success story
- Your entrepreneur experience story

For each story, read it aloud to someone or publish it if you feel comfortable enough to do so. These are stories you can carry with you moving forward in your life as a successful entrepreneur.

How was this experience? Even if you don't like to write, I think writing these stories opens up your creative juices and empowers you going forward.

Now, let's move on to the final step of the process, training for success.

LOSE YOUR SH*T

CHAPTER 9: STEP 6 – TRAIN FOR SUCCESS

"Much of the stress that people feel doesn't come from having too much to do. It comes from not finishing what they've started."

– David Allen

By now you should be feeling confident and free of so much pressure that was plaguing you when you started this process. You may even be on a real high! But how do you keep this going and not fall back into your old habits? Well, you have to train for it. Much like personal fitness training, I recommend "training for success," which includes an emotional fitness (e-fitness) accountability plan for regularly practicing the Lose-It method.

Preparing for Success

Because much may have changed for you during this journey, now is a good time to review and update the vision and goals of both your business and your life. I believe that having a clear vision is vital to your success in both your business and your life. I do "vision and goals" a bit different than most coaches. I have my clients create an intention statement that includes not only a vision for their future, but also their passions and dreams, including how they want to feel on a regular basis, for both their business and their life. When you are an entrepreneur, they go hand in hand. This intention statement will serve as your north star.

In my experience, a great intention statement does the following:

- Includes where you see yourself and your business in the future (5-10 years), that is, what you and your business will accomplish or contribute to in the future

- Is written clearly and concisely in the present tense (as if it was already true)
- Focuses on your passion and values – what is really important to you. Review the passions you identified earlier and ensure that they are reflected in your vision in some way.
- Includes something about your environment. (For example, where are you living? what is working environment like?)
- Is inspirational and includes how you and your business will change the world for the better

A Sample Intention Statement:

I am an entrepreneur and leader of extremely successful online business with offices and employees all over the world. My business has a positive impact on the world and my employees love me. I get to travel for business and pleasure. I have a happy, peaceful relationship with my family. My life is joyful and adventurous.

The Accountability Plan

Once you have your intention statement nailed, you are ready to create an accountability plan on how you will achieve that intention and how you will ensure your success and your continued emotional fitness as a true leader in your company, industry, and the world!

Your accountability plan might consist of the following:

1. Your intention statement that you wrote earlier.

2. Your success measures: come up with three to five things that would ensure that you had reached your intention. Add timeframes if you want. Think big!

3. A trigger/reaction/solution matrix as a reference to help you with daily triggers. (See sample below.)

4. A list of your regular practices that you want to engage in regularly, like:
   o Writing or updating your stories as they come up
   o Out of Body activities (getting the sh*t out of your body)
   o Out of Head activities (getting the sh*t out of your head)
   o Supervillain/superhero talks
   o Self-care practices (like meditation, yoga, walking in nature, etc.)
   o Your favorite sports or movement practices (like cycling, running, weight training, swimming, team sports)
   o Happiness/joy activities (what brings you joy, like listening to music, dancing, going to see comedy shows, singing karaoke)
   o Creative practices (like writing, drawing, painting, singing, playing music, performing, etc.)
   o Business nurturing practices (like a written blog or video blog series, speaking engagements)

5. A schedule of when you want to do the above. Maybe some every day, once a week, once a month, whatever works for you. Adjust as you go.

6. Update as needed.

Sample Accountability Plan

1. My sample intention statement: I am a wildly successful author, speaker, educator, and entrepreneur with a unique coaching business, online programs, and centers all over the world. My work has a ripple effect on the world, making it a better place. My life is in flow and full of adventure. I am calm, peaceful, and full of light and joy.

2. My success measures:

   o My latest book is a best seller on Amazon and the NYT. It has sold over a million copies. (1 year)

   o I have a Ted Talk published online that has more than a million views. (2 years)

   o My programs and retreats are sold out and have a waiting list. (2 years)

   o I have launched centers in the U.S. and Europe.
   (5 years)

3. My sample trigger/reaction/solution matrix:

My triggers	My reactions	Solutions/counter measures
Being the center of attention	Freeze, get anxious, nervous, stress goes way up	• Go for a walk in nature • Spend time with my dog • Grounding meditation • Head Workout or Fear Inventory • Dance Break
Being asked to do something that I do not want to do	Feel obligated. Hold back, do not set a boundary, rage and resentment start to build	• Boundaries Excuse List • Head Workout • Things Left Unsaid • The Purge + Jump for Joy • Go for a walk in nature • Play basketball, spin class • Supervillain/Superhero talk • Shame Inventory/The Shame
Being asked to present at conference	Fear, anxiety, panic, freeze, distraction, procrastination, insomnia	• Go for a walk in nature • Spend time with my dog • Grounding meditation, 3-body check in • Head Workout or Fear Inventory • Criticism Roleplay • Presentation Challenge • Vulnerability Challenge • The Scream + Jump for Joy • Dance Break

4. A list of my regular practices, along with desired frequency:
   - Out of Body activities:
     - The Purge – once a week
     - The Scream – twice a week
     - Dance Break – every day
     - The Shame – once a month
   - Out of Head activities:
     - The Head Workout or Fear Inventory– once a week
     - Things Left Unsaid – once a month
     - Shame Inventory – once a month
   - Supervillain/superhero talks:
     - Supervillain inquisition – once a week
     - Superhero vs Supervillain talk – once a month
   - Self-care practices:
     - Grounding meditation – once a day
     - Restorative yoga – once a week
     - Walking in nature – three times a week
   - My favorite sports or movement practices:
     - Walking – every day
     - Weight training – twice a week
     - Swimming laps at the gym – twice a week
   - My happiness/joy activities :
     - Listening to live music – once a month
     - Dancing – every day (dance break)
     - Jumping for joy – three times a week
     - Going to see comedy shows – once a quarter

- My creative practices
  - Writing – blogging two times a week
  - Learning to play piano – TBD
  - My business nurture practices
  - Written blog – twice a week
  - Vlog – every other day for engagement
  - Speaking engagements – submit to speak once a month

Of course you can make any kind of accountability document or plan that works for you. Once you get the hang of it, you can adjust your plan accordingly.. If you are a part of the Lose-It program, we have a few accountability options to help keep you on track.

We have come to the end of the Lose-It method. It has been quite a journey! How do you feel now? Do you feel less pressure? Do you feel emotionally fit? Do you feel like you can handle whatever stress comes your way? Are you living in flow with your life and your business? Do you feel more relaxed, more creative, more confident, more of a leader now? Are you interested in learning what is next? If so, move forward.

CHAPTER 10: BUST THROUGH TO THE OTHER SIDE

"When we long for life without difficulties, remind us that oaks grow strong in contrary winds and diamonds are made under pressure."

– Peter Marshall

Method Review

Now that we have come to the end of the process, let's do a recap of the Lose-It method.

1. **L – Learn Your Character Type**

   You learned your Character Type, what type of leader you are, how you handle stress and why.

2. **O – Own Your Challenges**

   You learned more about your type and its challenges. You outlined your current challenges, including your stress triggers and your reactions/defenses to those triggers and wrote them down.

3. **S – Shed Your Stories**

    You learned that usually when a stress response gets triggered, it comes from the "stories in our head," based on some memory of an event from your past. Here you identified those stories, wrote them down to get them out of your head, then documented any recurring or limiting beliefs to let them go. You created your own inner supervillain to support you in this step.

4. **E – Express Your Stress**

    Knowing the source of your stories and limiting beliefs really helped you connect the dots and brought your stress, your emotions to the surface (in case they weren't already there). In this step, you learned practices to effectively release your stress by fully expressing your thoughts and your emotions and clearing them out of your head and your body.

5. **I – Ignite Your Superpowers**

    In this step, you identified the "superpowers" that you want to ignite and own as a leader moving forward. You created your own inner superhero to support you in this. You also used your superhero to validate your goals and passions.

6. **T – Train for Success**

    In this final step, you created your intention and an accountability plan of how you will measure success and regularly use the practices in this program to ensure your continued emotional fitness so that you can be the true leader the world needs you to be.

This Is Hard Work

No doubt the Lose-It Method is hard. Looking at yourself and facing your challenges, stresses, victim stories and limiting beliefs does not come easy. Most people cannot even do that without quitting. Most of us spend our whole lives ignoring them or running away from them and just doing what we think we are "supposed to do" or what we learned to do. But how was that working out? Not so good, right? It's like going through life feeling like a victim, like you have no control. Remember in the movie Alien toward the end when Ripley (Sigourney Weaver) tries to escape the alien creature by sneaking away on the shuttle? But as soon as she got "comfortable" thinking she was safe... there it was... the demon was on the shuttle with her! She could not get rid of it until she battled it face-to-face. That is the same thing with your stress, challenges, triggers, demons, whatever you want to call them. Coming face-to-face with them (identifying them), figuring out where they came from, and then tackling them is the only way to get rid of them or disempower them from holding you back in your life. It is the only way to make a clear path for your rise to become the leader you were meant to be.

Stumbling Blocks

So how did you do? Did you complete the whole process? Or did you have some bumps in the road? If you did, you are not alone. Some common stumbling blocks include:

- "I am not sure what type I am. I think I am more than one." This is very common and not to worry as most people are more than one character type and you can change as you grow.

- "I have so many triggers and reactions that it's a bit overwhelming." This is also very common. Focusing on just a small number at a time is the key. One challenge at a time.

- "I did the supervillain thing, but I didn't get useful answers." Most of the time, this is due to not using a physical representation of your supervillain (very important) or not having a witness. Relax and be patient with yourself, and trust that all the answers are within you.

- "Trying to do the Out of Body exercises was very challenging. It is embarrassing if anyone can see or hear me." This is so common and understandable. Explaining to family members or roommates what you are doing and getting their cooperation is key. In fact, ask them to join in if they wish! They will reap amazing benefits if they do.

- "Putting an accountability plan in place was very hard. I need accountability!" Yes, accountability is key. Have a partner really helps with this. Someone to hold you accountable. Accountability is one of the best benefits of being a part of the Lose-It program.

Randy's Story

If you do make it through the whole process, you will reap so many rewards from it – in your life, your health, your relationships, and your business. It changes everything in your life. Let's look at the before and after of my client Randy.

When I first started with Randy, he was about to explode from the pressure of his business, his ex-wife, his mother, his daughter, and so on. His company was losing sales and he felt like every decision had to be run by him and he was exhausted. He said he felt like a tormented soul and a pressure cooker. He was highly anxious and easily agitated. He had high blood pressure, didn't sleep much, drank too much, and was about 50 pounds overweight. He hated that everyone wanted a piece of him. All he wanted was some time and space to just chill. He said that if he didn't get a handle on it, he was going to "lose it" and/or his company. He felt like he was on the brink of losing his reputation with his employees, which added to his anxiety and stress. He had previously lost a job because he had an outburst at work with his boss. He blamed it on his boss and the atmosphere there. He did not realize that he (his type is Endurer) had a hard time processing his emotions (mainly anger).

Once he learned about his type, his triggers, and reactions and created his inner supervillain, he was all in. He talks to supervillain all the time to get answers to issues that come up from day to day. He says, "It is very freeing to know that he is a part of me but not the real me. I have learned to talk to him and calm him (and me) down in almost every tense situation. I have not had an outburst since then." Randy also practices the Purge on a regular basis to get that built up anger out of his body. He practices it as his supervillain, which makes it so much easier. He said it was the freest he has felt in his whole life.

He now plays basketball on the weekends, something he had not done in a long time. Since we worked together, he has lost 30 pounds, his blood pressure is no longer a problem, he gets plenty of sleep, his relationships with both his mom and his ex have greatly improved, and he no longer dreads being around them. His employees love him, he created a new vision for his company, his sales are now way up so he has hired new staff, he learned to delegate, and now he actually has more free time to spend with his daughter. He has been asked to be on two boards and is now speaking at events in his industry. He now has the process, practices, and tools to handle whatever is thrown at him. He's even thinking about putting his staff through the program!

Maria's Story

Let me tell you about Maria who came to me last year. She was extremely overworked and undervalued at work. She had started her own business on the side but was afraid to quit her regular job and "go for it." Her new business was her passion but her job gave her "security." It provided no fulfillment to her at all. Her anxiety was very high. She was in her 50's and said to me, "Jodi, I am terrified that it is too late to live the life of my dreams. I don't know what to do. I hate my job and I feel so stuck." We agreed we were a fit to work together, but she was afraid to spend the money at that time. She put it off and said, "Let's do it next year."

In less than six months, her company's stock went down and they laid off their most expensive workers (mainly women over 50), including her. She got laid off, wasn't prepared financially for that, got desperate and took a worse job, working more hours and making less money, and now she is more miserable than ever. She completely put her business to the side. She gained 20 pounds, and her anxiety, frustration, and anger have gotten so bad that her daughter has stopped speaking to her! I've reached out to her, and I am hoping she will get back to me so we can work together because I know I can help her.

Because this process is so hard, not everyone completes it or sticks with it. At least, not without help or guidance. But the right guidance is key. I was in traditional talk therapy for well over a decade and it was not helping me anymore. It certainly did not help my stress level at all. It made it worse because I was stuck in a loop telling the same stories (the stories in my head) over and over but getting nowhere. It was not until I went to Lionheart and started working with mind-body practitioners that I truly started to transform my challenges (my demons) into something that supported me instead of hindered me. After that, connecting the dots between characterology and stress patterns, and subsequently getting the "sh*t" out of my head and my body. It was not an overnight process. It took some time, but the results were immediate and powerful.

That is why I designed the Lose-It program to go with the book. Everyone's journey is unique, and you are not meant to go through this alone. So many of the practices and activities in the process are meant to be done in the presence of another person, a guide.

When I first work with someone, I guide them through the whole process. I customize the activities and I hold them accountable for every step of the process. It is hard but it is SO rewarding at the same time. And it can be really fun as well. I work with individuals (1x1), groups and teams.

Alright, it is time to move on to the final chapter: Free to Lead.

CHAPTER 11: FREE TO LEAD

"You are braver than you believe and stronger than you seem and smarter than you think."

– Christopher Robin

We have reached the end of our journey together. At least, we have book-wise. This is the part that makes me sad. I want to stay connected with all of my readers and program participants. I hope you have enjoyed the process and even had fun along the way!

You are now armed with the following to help you on your continued journey to stress-free leadership:

- Your Character Type
- Your current challenges, stresses, triggers, reactions, and defenses
- Your original "stories in your head"
- Your inner supervillain (my favorite part!) and the inquisition
- Your documented limiting beliefs and the reverse beliefs to incorporate
- Tools to practice "expressing your stress" — getting the sh*t out of your head and your body
- Your inner superhero, your new passions, and your updated stories
- Your intention and your accountability plan with your list of practices you will continue and a schedule

Using these resources, you will be able to understand and handle the daily pressure put on you as a leader, easily release stress as it comes up, be more creative and productive, easily delegate tasks, and have time and energy left over to spend with your loved ones.

My Wish for You

My wish for you is that you now know how to decrease daily stress, effectively deal with your anxiety and anger, and achieve inner peace. That you have the ability to be free of feeling like a pressure cooker so that you can truly live in your zone of genius, own your superpowers, and be the leader you were meant to be. To be a role model, to effectively and calmly lead your business, your family and your community to make the world a better place. I desire for you not live in fear or anxiety or repressed anger or frustration. To not hide. To speak up for yourself and stand up for who you truly are and what you believe in. To truly pursue your passion and live the life you came to live.

What is Next?

I believe in you – you can do this. But you are not alone. If you feel that you need accountability or you feel like you need to go deeper, I invite you to investigate if the Lose-It Program is for you. If you fit any of the following descriptions, you are a candidate for the Lose-It Program:

- Your business/work is overwhelming to you and you never seem to be able to get ahead.
- Your anxiety level is very high and you are exhausted and overwhelmed.
- You feel responsible for everyone in your life.
- You have been told you have an anger or stress management problem.

- You are involved in every decision in your business or at your company and it is just too much!

- You feel like your reputation is slipping in your business and it is worrying you.

- You have health issues, such as high blood pressure, weight issues, depression, anxiety or exhaustion.

- You like the safety and security of working with someone who can guide you every step of the way.

Can you imagine your life if you could easily handle the daily pressure, release your toxic stress, and perform at your most creative, productive, and genius self? Imagine not being worried about being involved in every decision. Imagine having time and energy left over to go on vacations and spend with your loved ones. Is that something you want? If so, I can help you.

If you are interested in exploring our program, schedule a free discovery session. If you are struggling with stress as a leader or entrepreneur, don't hesitate to schedule a session and we can figure out the next best steps for you. Just go to the website at comealiveinstitute.com/contact/and select the **Schedule a Call** button. I look forward to working with you.

FURTHER READING ON CHARACTER TYPES

The 5 Personality Patterns by Steven Kessler

The Undefended Self by Susan Thesenga

Healing Developmental Trauma by Laurence Heller and Aline LaPierre

The Language of the Body by Alexander Lowen

Hands of Light by Barbara Ann Brennan

Light Emerging by Barbara Ann Brennan

Character Analysis by Wilhelm Reich

ACKNOWLEDGMENTS

There are so many people who helped make this book happen. I first want to thank two of my closest friends, Melani Meyer and Donna Synodis, who have believed in me and supported me every step of the way in my amazing journey. I could not have done this without you. I want to thank Marty Avary for being my true sister through both Lionheart and Mama Gena's and so much more. I want to thank my dear friend, Cynthia Savelli, who has always supported me no matter what. I want to thank Rudy McCallum for always being there to support me and for his feedback on much of the content for the book. I want to thank Laura Bartlett for all of the feedback she gave me on the book and more. I want to thank all of my Lionheart teachers, who were so brilliant and fierce in their teachings, coaching, and healing – Dan Buffo, Laura Fine, Deb Allen, Scott Bader, Sandra Pribanic, Nino Sekopet, and Sheryl Grant. I especially want to call out Dan Buffo for helping me heal my adrenal exhaustion and Deb Allen for her undying support and her amazing women's circles she holds around the world. I want to thank Kadena Tate Simon for being the best business coach, friend and marketing genius. Your constant support means so much to me. I want to thank Regena Thomashauer for creating such an amazing program and community of women. I want to thank my close "sister goddess" friends who supported me through this journey, most especially Terri-Marie Assous, Debra Keaton, Julia Vasquez, Valerie Bennis, and Mikelle Terson. I want to thank all of my clients who provided so much insight. I want to thank my personal trainer Chris Weigel for constantly reminding me to live a life of passion while I was his client and believing in me. I want to thank Angela Lauria and everyone at the Author Incubator. And last but certainly not least, I want to thank both of my amazing editors, Bethany Davis and Moriah Richard. Thank you for your support and valuable feedback. I could not have done it without you.

ABOUT THE AUTHOR

Jodi Hadsell is an emotional fitness coach, crisis coach, and passion archaeologist. She is the founder of the Come Alive Institute where she specializes in helping entrepreneurs, businesses, leaders and individuals not only survive but thrive in crisis.

Jodi has spent her entire career in service to helping people improve their lives. For over 20 years she worked in corporate learning and development, training and coaching employees in some of the largest technology companies in the world, including EDS, Apple, AT&T and SAP.

She has designed and facilitated dozens of successful training programs throughout her career, from new hire training to leadership development. She has been a speaker at MacWorld, Human Capital Institute (HCI), and

Association of Talent Development (ATD) conferences on talent and career development.

While working in the corporate world, Jodi completed years of intense study in mind-body therapy and received three mind-body certifications. In 2011 she began her mind-body therapy practice and crisis coaching, where she has helped dozens of clients through a deep transformation to conquer stress and live the life they came here to live.

In 2018 Jodi finally decided to leave the corporate world to publish her first book, Come Alive: Find Your Passion, Change Your Life, Change the World, and an accompanying program so that she could help as many people as possible transform their lives and find their true passion.

In 2020 she knew she needed to step up to the moment and write this book and develop an accompanying program for entrepreneurs. She also has a podcast on YouTube where she interviews entrepreneurs and experts to discuss solutions to stress-related issues called Come Alive with Jodi Hadsell.

Jodi currently lives in Dallas, TX, but her wanderlust takes her to foreign lands frequently.

Website: comealiveinstitute.com
Email: info@comealiveinstitute.com
Facebook: facebook.com/youcomealive
LinkedIn: https://www.linkedin.com/company/come-alive-institute
YouTube: https://www.youtube.com/channel/UCaeMBnmTMlVpMeXEFSopvag

THANK YOU

Thank you for reading my book! I would love to hear more about your experience and your stress-defeating journey as an entrepreneur or leader. Please email me at jodi@comealiveinstitute.com.

Share Your Success

If you go through the process (either through the book or program), I invite you to share your success on our Facebook group. Sharing your success can help you as well as others who are in the process.

Free Discovery Session

If you are interested in exploring deeper or are curious about our program, schedule a free discovery session. If you are struggling with stress as a leader or entrepreneur, don't hesitate to contact me for a strategy session and we can figure out the next best steps for you Just go to the website at comealiveinstitute.com/contact/and select the **Schedule a Call** button. I look forward to hearing from you.

LinkedIn: https://www.linkedin.com/in/jodihadsell/
Instagram: https://www.instagram.com/jodihadsell/
Facebook: fb.me/youcomealive
YouTube:
https://www.youtube.com/channel/UCaeMBnmTMlVpMe XEFSopvag